Serving a Crucified King

SERVING A CRUCIFIED KING

*Meditations on Faith, Politics,
and the Unyielding Pursuit of God's Reign*

JESSE STEVEN WHEELER

Foreword by *Michael F. Kuhn*

RESOURCE *Publications* · Eugene, Oregon

SERVING A CRUCIFIED KING
Meditations on Faith, Politics, and the Unyielding Pursuit of God's Reign

Copyright © 2021 Jesse Steven Wheeler. All rights reserved. Except for brief quotations in critical publications or reviews, no part of this book may be reproduced in any manner without prior written permission from the publisher. Write: Permissions, Wipf and Stock Publishers, 199 W. 8th Ave., Suite 3, Eugene, OR 97401.

Resource Publications
An Imprint of Wipf and Stock Publishers
199 W. 8th Ave., Suite 3
Eugene, OR 97401

www.wipfandstock.com

PAPERBACK ISBN: 978-1-6667-0958-2
HARDCOVER ISBN: 978-1-6667-2185-0
EBOOK ISBN: 978-1-6667-2186-7

OCTOBER 28, 2021 2:54 PM

For
Jesse Nimer ("Nimer")
Thomas Elias ("Tommy")
James Issa ("Jamie")
Heidi Miriam

"In everything do to others as you would have them do to you; for this is the law and the prophets."

—Matthew 7:12 (NRSV)

Cover Image: "Christ Pantocrator" in the dome of *catholicon* of the Church of the Holy Sepulchre, Jerusalem, Palestine, traditional site of the death and resurrection of Jesus

Contents

Permissions | xi
Foreword | xiii
Preface | xv

1. The Empathy Imperative | 1
2. True Worship | 3
3. Thy Kingdom Come | 6
4. For the World | 9
5. Why Sabbath? | 11
6. The Stranger | 14
7. Every Tear | 17
8. Supremely Good | 20
9. Religion: Pure & Faultless | 23
10. Kingdom Economics 101 | 26
11. Kingdom Economics 102 | 29
12. Joy, Justice, & Peace | 32
13. Seek the Peace | 35
14. The Peacemakers | 37
15. Even the Gentiles | 39
16. Flipping the Script | 41
17. Such as These | 43
18. The One Who Sent Me | 45
19. Defacing the Image of God | 47
20. In Their Power | 50

21	Farmers & Firearms	53
22	What God Wants	55
23	Those on His Right	57
24	As One Who Had Authority	59
25	Salty Torchbearers	61
26	Yes. No. Maybe?	64
27	The Tyranny of Approval	67
28	Keeping Up with the Kingdom	70
29	Look. Notice. Desire.	73
30	Drink the Cup	76
31	As I Have Done	79
32	The Same Attitude	82
33	Prayer as Political	84
34	Misplaced Allegiances	86
35	Tested Loyalties	89
36	Blind to Our Blindness	92
37	A Holy Kiss	94
38	Empathy Embodied	97
39	There Are Two Ways	100
40	Worship as Farce	102
41	Magic Pools of Water	105
42	Bad Theology Kills	108
43	Worthless Assemblies	111
44	The Great Reversal	113
45	Willing to Listen	116
46	#FarTooManyMen	119
47	A Good Man	121
48	Mary Knew	124
49	The Root of Jesse	127
50	Into Practice	129

Palm Sunday: The Triumphal Entry | 132
Holy Monday: Overturning Tables | 135
Holy Tuesday: What Belongs to God | 138
Spy Wednesday: Unholy Alliances | 141
Maundy Thursday: By the Sword | 145
Good Friday: The Crucified King | 148
Great and Holy Saturday: I Saw a Lamb | 151
Easter Sunday: New Creation | 155

Appendix | 159
Bibliography | 165

Permissions

Scripture quotations marked NIV are taken from The Holy Bible, New International Version® NIV®, Copyright © 1973, 1978, 1984, 2011 by Biblica, Inc.™. Used by permission. All rights reserved worldwide.

Scripture quotations marked NLT are taken from the Holy Bible, New Living Translation, Copyright © 1996, 2004, 2015 by Tyndale House Foundation. Used by permission of Tyndale House Publishers, Carol Stream, Illinois 60188. All rights reserved.

Scripture quotations marked CEB are taken from the Common English Bible, Copyright © 2011. Used by permission. All rights reserved.

Scripture quotations marked NRSV are taken from the New Revised Standard Version Bible, Copyright © 1989 the Division of Christian Education of the National Council of the Churches of Christ in the United States of America. Used by permission. All rights reserved.

Scripture quotations marked CEV are taken from the Contemporary English Version, Copyright © 1991, 1992, 1995 by American Bible Society. Used by permission.

Scripture quotations marked ESV are taken from the ESV® Bible (The Holy Bible, English Standard Version®), Copyright © 2001 by Crossway, a publishing ministry of Good News Publishers. Used by permission. All rights reserved.

Scripture quotations marked NKJV are taken from the New King James Version®, Copyright © 1982 by Thomas Nelson. Used by permission. All rights reserved.

This work includes numerous public domain quotations and prayers from historical Christian figures, selections from the 1979 Episcopal *Book of Common Prayer*, and brief scriptural citations from the Douay-Rheims Bible (DRB) and the Open English Bible (OEB).

Foreword

FOUR GAPS

I was raised in an evangelical home. While I am grateful for a strong biblical foundation, the years have uncovered some gaps in my Christian upbringing. I'm still learning about those and the book you're now reading has brought many of those to mind. They include:

- *An individualist spirituality*: I became proficient at the "quiet time." My day always began (still does) with some time alone in God's word and prayer. Well and good but, unconsciously, that became a spiritual thermometer. I assessed my spiritual maturity based on that spiritual discipline practiced in isolation.

- *An otherworld eschatology*: I believed in the afterlife and understood that things would not be made right until Jesus returned. Unconsciously, I imbibed a "heaven is over yonder" mentality. The song "This world is not my home / I'm only passing through"[1] gives away my Appalachian upbringing but also reveals a serious gap in my understanding of God's purposes for creation and humanity.

- *A laissez-faire attitude towards politics*: Jesus's teaching left me skeptical about what is today called "Christian nationalism." In fact, a pietistic outlook led me to deflect political involvement. Aware of greed, I hoped that Christian influence in a capitalist society was a sufficient corrective. I was into "spiritual transformation." Getting people introduced to Jesus was what mattered.

- *A social exclusivity*: America's prohibition of slavery inoculated me to the evils of contemporary racism. The displacement of indigenous

1. Traditional

Foreword

people was an unfortunate but closed chapter in my history book. I never considered that my community was implicated in the collective sins of the past. I wanted good Christian leaders to enforce a biblical morality on society. A generous dose of patriarchy colored my outlook.

I am not the only one. My experience is not unlike other evangelicals who, skeptical of a "social gospel," step away from engagement in society and public policy. The other alternative, more prominent today, is equally deleterious—enforcing social change by overpowering political adversaries through legislation and the ballot box.

This book proposes a third way—an engagement in public life by tenaciously following a crucified Lord. It echoes the prophetic cry for justice as integral and essential to our witness in the world. It resonates with Jesus's mandate:

> *The Spirit of the Lord is upon me because he has anointed me to proclaim good news to the poor. He has sent me to proclaim liberty to the captives and recovering of sight to the blind, to set at liberty those who are oppressed, to proclaim the year of the Lord's favor.*[2]

As a recovering pietist evangelical, I heartily recommend this book. The prayers and readings conspire to move us beyond a laissez-faire isolation into a real-world discipleship. The additional resources at the end of each entry form a rich library for a growth that is rooted in following Jesus in the public square.

Having known and worked with Jesse Wheeler in Lebanon, I know this book grows out of his heart. Well-attuned to the inconsistencies of an other-worldly spirituality, Jesse combines Scripture with contributions from past Christian spokespersons. The result is a clarion call back to the real work of being a disciple of Jesus in our society. Expect to have your thinking challenged, your heart moved, and your action re-oriented.

Michael F. Kuhn, PhD
International Theological Education Network
Author of *God Is One: A Christian Defence of Divine Unity in the Muslim Golden Age*

---

2. Luke 4:18–19 (ESV).

Preface

THINGS SPIRITUAL AND SOCIO-POLITICAL ALIKE

The origins of this collection lay in a series of daily social media devotions born out of the confluence of the COVID-19 pandemic, a frighteningly polarized political environment surrounding the US presidential election, and the 2020 Lenten season. During that time of anxiety and heightened sensitivity to things spiritual and socio-political alike, I began to share—with intentionally minimal commentary—those passages of Scripture that have been most influential in shaping my theo-political outlook, seeking to shine the light of God's word upon our particularly troubled historical moment. The meditations contained herein reflect an outworking and expansion of that original aim, especially as many of those initial sensitivities and anxieties have become all the more urgent and that much greater.

Moreover, this collection speaks to a much deeper set of problems within the contemporary church, problems of misplaced allegiance and misguided discipleship. If Jesus Christ is who we claim him to be, then we must ask ourselves if we are truly conducting our lives and constructing our communities in light of that astonishing reality. Offering an answer to this question, in what are among the most personally transformative paragraphs I have ever read, Christian ethicists Glen Stassen and David Gushee write,

> Christianity is a nonsensical enterprise apart from Jesus, its central figure, its source, ground, authority, and destiny.
> Here is the problem. Christian churches across the theological and confessional spectrum . . . are often guilty of evading Jesus, the cornerstone and center of the Christian faith. Specifically, *the teachings and practices of Jesus*—especially the largest block of his teaching, the Sermon on the Mount—are routinely ignored

Preface

or misinterpreted in the preaching and teaching ministry of the churches and in Christian scholarship and ethics. This evasion of the concrete ethical teachings of Jesus has seriously malformed Christian moral practices, moral beliefs, and moral witness. Jesus taught that the test of our discipleship is whether we act on his teachings, whether we "put into practice" his words. This is what it means to "buil[d our] house on rock" (Matthew 7:24).

We believe Jesus meant what he said. And so it is no overstatement to claim that the evasion of the teachings of Jesus constitutes a crisis of Christian identity and raises the question of who exactly is functioning as the Lord of the church. When Jesus's way of discipleship is thinned down, marginalized, or avoided, then churches and Christians lose their antibodies against infection by secular ideologies that manipulate Christians into serving the purposes of some other lord. We fear precisely that kind of idolatry now.[1]

The tragic events of January 6, 2021, in Washington, DC, where the cross of Christ stood much too comfortably alongside the gallows pole and the Confederate battle flag, was simply the most recent manifestation of this long-standing crisis of faith. I absolutely believe that the Holy Spirit is present within and among his people, transforming lives and restoring communities, such that nothing can or will stand in the way of his purposes on earth. But, as long as the contemporary church continues to act in a manner so seemingly at odds with the mission and message of Jesus, it remains in a state of emergency. Albeit a serious charge, solving this crisis is of the utmost importance if we are to live once again in faithful obedience to Jesus Christ, as king. For the magnitude of the problem necessitates the establishment of a movement of kingdom citizens devoted to the cruciform reign of Christ and committed to a wholesale transformation in thinking and practice within the church.

Meanwhile, there are those who seek to live out the demands of Scripture by calling attention to and attempting to address such apparent contradictions, yet are accused instead of acting in a manner contrary to, or at least inconsistent with, "the Christian worldview"—as divisive, dissident liberals, Marxists, or even ungodly heretics. Famously, it was the Brazilian Catholic Archbishop Hélder Câmara who called out this dynamic while declaring, "When I give food to the poor, they call me a saint. When I ask why they are poor, they call me a communist."[2] Building upon this senti-

---

1. Stassen and Gushee, *Kingdom Ethics*, xvi.
2. Câmara, *Essential Writings*, 11.

ment for our current moment, my friend and former colleague Jonathan Walton of KTF (Keeping the Faith) Press echoes Câmara when he writes,

> I want to live out Matthew 25, so I'm called a Marxist. I want to be faithful to Galatians 2–3 so I'm asked about "Critical Race Theory." I believe we should love our neighbors by providing for them the way I've been provided for so I'm a "Socialist."
>
> Call me what you will. I'm grateful that Jesus will call me by my name and call his own on judgment day. After all, justice is a God concept—not a product of Marxism, Socialism, or Critical Race Theory.[3]

For it is precisely what I consider to be my theological conservatism—my fidelity to Jesus, to the authority of the Bible, and to an unrelenting pursuit of God's reign on earth as it is in heaven—that results in what might be perceived by others as an apparent political-economic progressivism. Nevertheless, we must never succumb to the temptations of partisanship subsumed to the interests of the contemporary powers that be—left, right, or center—even if I am of the conviction that all religion is inherently political. Our firm foundation is upon the rock of the one true king Jesus Christ, his authoritative teachings and cruciform example, as witnessed to in the pages of Scripture.

READ, REFLECT, PRAY, EXPLORE

The devotionals contained in these pages were designed with both personal and group study in mind, alongside a focus on simplicity and flexibility of use. As found, each meditation is organized according to a straightforward pattern of *Read, Reflect, Pray, and Explore*:

- *Read* constitutes the bulk of a day's reflection, consisting of a particular passage (or passages) of Scripture followed by a short commentary on the meaning and message of the selection as it relates to the intersection of faith, politics, and the reign of God.
- *Reflect* is composed of two or more questions focused on an understanding of the reading and the implications of living it out within individual, community, or socio-cultural contexts.

---

3. Walton, Facebook, December 17, 2020.

Preface

- *Pray* consists of a time for praise, confession, thanksgiving, petition, intercession, and simply spending time with God. Spanning the breadth of church history, each devotional includes the selection of a written prayer associated with the day's theme. Archaic language has been updated as needed for use as a contemporary devotional.
- *Explore* contains a series of recommendations for those interested in pursuing a specific topic in greater depth.

Occasionally, you will find a break with the above formula in favor of a more overtly meditative and prayerful reading of a passage.

The *Read, Reflect, Pray, and Explore* pattern is particularly suited to individual study, though it can readily serve as the basis for group study or teaching as well. For this reason, I have included within an appendix a brief introduction to four great methods for adapting these meditations to a longer weekly format. They include:

- Inductive Bible Study
- Discovery Bible Study
- HBLT ("Hook, Book, Look, Took")
- Lectio Divina

Serving a Crucified King contains fifty numbered devotions plus an additional seven without numbers coinciding with Holy Week. These can be added to the sequence whenever Holy Week comes along or read in their current position as a conclusion to the devotional series at any time in the year.

A BRIEF NOTE ON SOURCES AND INFLUENCES

In an effort to facilitate readability and ease of use, I have intentionally chosen to limit the use of footnotes within this collection. So, while the words may be my own—unless otherwise indicated—I am entirely dependent upon the witness of scholars, pastors, practitioners, and women and men of faith far wiser than myself. The phenomenal resources listed in the *Explore* subsections, as well as the bibliography, will point you in the direction of those voices on whom I am dependent. However, I must state upfront that I am especially indebted to the following:

Preface

- Glen H. Stassen and David P. Gushee's groundbreaking *Kingdom Ethics: Following Jesus in Contemporary Context* (currently in its second edition) is a "top of the pile" resource I have visited time and again as an educator, author, and intermittent preacher. I am also quite fond of Stassen's *Living the Sermon on the Mount: A Practical Hope for Grace and Deliverance* as a popular introduction to his ethical thinking. Stassen's influence can be found echoed through this entire collection.

- Kenneth E. Bailey's *Jesus Through Middle Eastern Eyes: Cultural Studies in the Gospels* is a brilliant, culturally- and historically-informed analysis of the life and teachings of Jesus.

- George Eldon Ladd's *A Theology of the New Testament*, as revised and expanded by my former professor, Donald Hagner, is likewise an indispensable resource.

- The many works of N.T. Wright. *Simply Jesus: A New Vision of Who He Is, Who He Was, What He Did, and Why He Matters*, and *How God Became King: The Forgotten Story of the Gospels* stand out as particularly relevant.

- As you will see, I have also drawn inspiration from the extraordinary prayers of late nineteenth and early twentieth century Baptist pastor, activist, and theologian Walter Rauschenbusch as found in *For God and the People: Prayers of the Social Awakening*, alongside the consistently beautiful prayers of the episcopal *Book of Common Prayer* (1979).

ACKNOWLEDGEMENTS

Finally, I am forever indebted to Michael F. Kuhn, Suzie Schenkel Lahoud, and Celeste M. Wheeler, whose invaluable insight, feedback, and encouragement have been instrumental in helping me transform a haphazard assortment of social media posts into something a publisher would be willing to print. I am especially grateful to Heidi Miriam Wheeler, the love of my life, and to our three incredible boys for their extraordinary support, patience, and understanding through the duration of this project. I stand in awe of Heidi's eagle-eyed proofreading.

1

The Empathy Imperative

As we attempt to navigate the troubled waters of Christian faith and politics, most significant for helping us find our bearings and guiding us safely through are the following words of Jesus:

> *In everything do to others as you would have them do to you; for this is the law and the prophets.*
> —Matthew 7:12 (NRSV)

Known popularly as the Golden Rule, this modest teaching is so central to the mission and message of Jesus that the book of James actually speaks of it as the royal law. It is the law of King Jesus. In fact, the entirety of Scripture is encapsulated by this injunction to "do for others what you would have them do for you." It is a summons to picture oneself in the place and circumstances of another, a posture otherwise referred to as *empathy*. Embodied in the very person of Christ Jesus, such empathy is all encompassing. For the Lordship of Christ, and therefore his instruction to us, encompasses all areas of life, both within and beyond the walls of the church, be it personal or political, inter-communal or economic. As Dutch theologian and statesman Abraham Kuyper once proclaimed, "There is not a square inch in the whole domain of our human existence over which Christ, who is sovereign over all, does not cry, mine!"[1] Ultimately, our imperative as would-be ambassadors of King Jesus—in everything and at all times!—is the pursuit and practice of empathy.

---

1. Mouw, *Kuyper*, Chap. 1.

REFLECT

- To what extent does the mandate to "do to others what you would have them do to you" inform your understanding and practice of faithful, Christ-centered living?
- How might a commitment to the practice of empathy look if pursued in a specific area of your life, "be it personal or political, intercommunal or economic?" Choose a particular domain and consider the implications.

PRAY

Steer the ship of my life, good Lord, to your quiet harbor, where I can be safe from the storms of sin and conflict. Show me the course I should take. Renew in me the gift of discernment, so that I can always see the right direction in which I should go. And give me the strength and the courage to choose the right course, even when the sea is rough and the waves are high, knowing that through enduring hardship and danger in your name we shall find comfort and peace.

—Basil of Caesarea (fourth century)

EXPLORE

Himes, Brant M. *For a Better Worldliness: Abraham Kuyper, Dietrich Bonhoeffer, and Discipleship for the Common Good.* Eugene: Pickwick, 2019.

Mouw, Richard J. *Abraham Kuyper: A Short and Personal Introduction.* Grand Rapids: Eerdmans, 2011.

2

True Worship

THE FOLLOWING EXHORTATION PRESENTS US with a revolutionary understanding of the heart of God and of his expectations for us. As revealed by the prophet Isaiah, we see that God would choose to forgo, or rather reject, our worship of him so long as we persist in fomenting violence, perpetuating injustice, and practicing exclusion:

> *For day after day they seek me out; they seem eager to know my ways, as if they were a nation that does what is right and has not forsaken the commands of its God. They ask me for just decisions and seem eager for God to come near them.*
>
> *"Why have we fasted," they say, "and you have not seen it? Why have we humbled ourselves, and you have not noticed?"*
>
> *Yet on the day of your fasting, you do as you please and exploit all your workers. Your fasting ends in quarreling and strife, and in striking each other with wicked fists. You cannot fast as you do today and expect your voice to be heard on high.*
>
> *Is this the kind of fast I have chosen, only a day for people to humble themselves? Is it only for bowing one's head like a reed and for lying in sackcloth and ashes? Is that what you call a fast, a day acceptable to the Lord?*
>
> *Is not this the kind of fasting I have chosen: to loose the chains of injustice and untie the cords of the yoke, to set the oppressed free and break every yoke? Is it not to share your food with the hungry and to provide the poor wanderer with shelter—when you see the naked, to clothe them, and not to turn away from your own flesh and blood?*
>
> *Then your light will break forth like the dawn, and your healing will quickly appear; then your righteousness will go before you, and*

the glory of the Lord will be your rear guard. Then you will call, and the Lord will answer; you will cry for help, and he will say: Here am I.

If you do away with the yoke of oppression, with the pointing finger and malicious talk, and if you spend yourselves in behalf of the hungry and satisfy the needs of the oppressed, then your light will rise in the darkness, and your night will become like the noonday.

The Lord will guide you always; he will satisfy your needs in a sun-scorched land and will strengthen your frame. You will be like a well-watered garden, like a spring whose waters never fail. Your people will rebuild the ancient ruins and will raise up the age-old foundations; you will be called Repairer of Broken Walls, Restorer of Streets with Dwellings.

—Isaiah 58:2–12 (NIV)

As individuals and communities of faith, we often long for revival. Hoping to reignite a feeling of passion or spiritual vibrancy, we take part in late-night praise gatherings, mountaintop prayer retreats, evangelistic and moral crusades, or charity drives. This is wonderful, so long as we are being transformed by our worship into the people whom God desires us to be. Yet, how often in our churchly pursuits do we neglect, downplay, or outright ignore our complicity in perpetuating the violence and injustice that too often defines our societies and, in doing so, sideline those transformative practices that would contribute to the very revival we seek? To what extent does our demand—for high-tech goods and high-yield investments, fresh coffee and fast fashion, affordable chocolate and inexpensive petroleum—implicate each of us in a global web of socio-economic injustice? But, we often fail to truly understand or even acknowledge the exploitative practices upon which many of our modern conveniences are based.

It is no secret, however, as to which transformative practices we are expected to proactively undertake, for the prophet Isaiah directs us to:

- Loose the chains of injustice,
- Untie the cords of the yoke,
- Set the oppressed free,
- Break every yoke,
- Share your food with the hungry, and
- Provide the poor wanderer with shelter.
- When you see the naked, to clothe them, and

- Not turn away from your own flesh and blood.
- Do away with the yoke of oppression,
- Do away with the pointing finger and malicious talk,
- Spend yourselves in behalf of the hungry, and
- Satisfy the needs of the oppressed.

"Then," and only then, the prophet tells us, "your light will break forth like the dawn, and your healing will quickly appear; then your righteousness will go before you, and the glory of the Lord will be your rear guard. Then you will call, and the Lord will answer; you will cry for help, and he will say: Here am I."

REFLECT

- In this passage, what does the prophet Isaiah reveal about the heart of God and his priorities for human society?
- Have you or your community ever been guilty of what might be considered "false worship?" How might a commitment to "true fasting," as described by the prophet, impact your personal discipleship, alongside the outlook and orientation of your faith community?

PRAY

> I pray for all those whom I have in any way grieved, vexed, oppressed, or scandalized, by word or deed, knowingly or unknowingly, that you may forgive all our sins and offences against each other. Take away, O Lord, from our hearts all suspiciousness, indignation, anger, and contention, and whatever is calculated to wound charity or to lessen love of others. Have mercy on me, O Lord; have mercy on all who seek your mercy; give grace to the needy; make us so to live that we may be found worthy to enjoy the fulfilment of your grace and attain to eternal life.
>
> —Thomas à Kempis (fifteenth century)

EXPLORE

Labberton, Mark. *The Dangerous Act of Worship: Living God's Call to Justice*. Downers Grove: IVP Books, 2007.
———. *The Dangerous Act of Loving Your Neighbor: Seeing Others through the Eyes of Jesus*. Downers Grove: IVP Books, 2010.

3

Thy Kingdom Come

THERE ARE MANY WHO FAITHFULLY believe in the atoning death and resurrection of Jesus, admirably loving, serving, and sacrificing time and treasure for the sake of God and others. This is as it should be. Nonetheless, far too many of us never received adequate instruction regarding the in-breaking kingdom of God and its absolute centrality to the mission and message of Christ. That this has been the case for so many is deeply troubling.

> *From that time on Jesus began to preach, "Repent, for the kingdom of heaven has come near."*
>
> —MATTHEW 4:17 (NIV)

> *May your kingdom come soon. May your will be done, on earth as it is in heaven.*
>
> —MATTHEW 6:10 (NLT)

> *The kingdom of heaven is like a mustard seed that someone took and planted in his field. It's the smallest of all seeds. But when it's grown, it's the largest of all vegetable plants. It becomes a tree so that the birds in the sky come and nest in its branches . . .*
> *The kingdom of heaven is like yeast, which a woman took and hid in a bushel of wheat flour until the yeast had worked its way through all the dough.*
>
> —MATTHEW 13:31–33 (CEB)

Few contemporary authors have spoken so prolifically with regard to the significance of God's reign "on earth as it is in heaven" as the always eloquent N. T. Wright. The whole gospel, he tells us,

> is the story of God's kingdom being launched on earth as it is in heaven, generating a new state of affairs in which the power of evil has been decisively defeated, the new creation has been decisively launched, and Jesus's followers have been commissioned and equipped to put that victory and that inaugurated new world into practice.[1]

As such, our collective failure to grasp the centrality of an already inaugurated—if not yet consummated—kingdom has been severely detrimental to the life and witness of the church. For if the locus of our perceived salvation lies beyond this material realm and solely within an individual's disembodied soul, then of what ultimate value is the health and well-being of the world we call home or of those persons and communities with whom we share it? Such thinking stands at odds with the worldview of the biblical authors, rendering much of the Bible either inconsequential or incomprehensible as a result. But, as Wright would later add, "Jesus's resurrection is the beginning of God's new project not to snatch people away from earth to heaven, but to colonize earth with the life of heaven. That, after all, is what the Lord's Prayer is about."[2]

REFLECT

- How have you and your faith community traditionally understood the meaning and significance of God's reign "on earth as it is in heaven?"
- How might a renewed focus on "colonizing earth with the life of heaven" impact our practice as followers of Christ—"be it personal or political, intercommunal or economic?"

PRAY

> *Christ, you have bidden us pray for the coming of your Father's kingdom, in which his righteous will shall be done on earth. We have treasured your words, but we have forgotten their meaning, and your great hope has grown dim in your church. We bless you for the inspired souls of all ages who saw afar the shining city of God, and*

---

1. Wright, *Hope*, 204.
2. Wright, *Hope*, 293.

by faith left the profit of the present to follow their vision. We rejoice that today the hope of these lonely hearts is becoming the clear faith of millions. Help us, O Lord, in the courage of faith to seize what has now come so near, that the glad day of God may dawn at last. As we have mastered nature that we might gain wealth, help us now to master the social relations of humankind that we may gain justice and a world of brothers and sisters.

For what shall it profit our nation if it gain numbers and riches, and lose the sense of the living God and the joy of human siblinghood? Make us determined to live by truth and not by lies, to found our common life on the eternal foundations of righteousness and love, and no longer to prop up the tottering house of wrong by legalized cruelty and force. Help us to make the welfare of all the supreme law of our land, that so our commonwealth may be built strong and secure on the love of all its citizens. Cast down the throne of Mammon who ever grinds the life of women and men, and set up your throne, O Christ, for you died that people might live. Show your erring children at last the way from the City of Destruction to the City of Love, and fulfil the longings of the prophets of humanity. Our master, once more we make your faith our prayer: "Thy kingdom come! Thy will be done on earth!"

—WALTER RAUSCHENBUSCH (1910)

EXPLORE

Wright, N. T. *Surprised by Hope: Rethinking Heaven, the Resurrection, and the Mission of the Church.* New York: HarperCollins, 2009.

4

For the World

IN THE FOLLOWING PASSAGE, JESUS Christ represents within himself the full authority of God's kingdom on earth as he stands face to face with the Roman military governor Pilate. Meanwhile, Pilate was himself the representative of Roman imperial dominance under the self-declared "god" Caesar. As presented by John, this is a scene of dramatic tension between two very different kingdoms, each with two very different kings:

> *Pilate went back into the palace. He summoned Jesus and asked, "Are you the king of the Jews?"*
>
> *Jesus answered, "Do you say this on your own or have others spoken to you about me?"*
>
> *Pilate responded, "I'm not a Jew, am I? Your nation and its chief priests handed you over to me. What have you done?"*
>
> *Jesus replied, "My kingdom doesn't originate from this world. If it did, my guards would fight so that I wouldn't have been arrested by the Jewish leaders. My kingdom isn't from here."*
>
> —JOHN 18:33–36 (CEB)

It is significant to note that while not *from*—or *of*—this world, the kingdom about which Jesus speaks remains very much *in* and "*for* this world."[1] I particularly appreciate this specific translation for just that reason. The kingdom may "originate" in heaven, but it certainly doesn't stay there. Understanding this seemingly minor, yet nevertheless essential, nuance provides a much-needed corrective to hyper-spiritualized notions of Christ's reign as often popularly understood. And, it reinforces the kingdom's practical relevance

---

1. Wright, *God Became King*, 241.

for our world. In fact, Jesus explains this contrast in distinctly practical terms, declaring that if his kingdom had been like those of this world, then his disciples would have fought to prevent his arrest. But, this happens to be a very different sort of kingdom, for the very thing which distinguishes the kingdom of Christ from those of this world (Rome for instance) is its categorical rejection of violence, domination, and retaliation. It's kingdom by way of cross. So, in his response to Pilate, Jesus simultaneously relativizes all human authority and casts judgement upon the means and methods by which that authority is so often exercised.

REFLECT

- How have you and your faith community understood Jesus's declaration that his kingdom is "not of this world?"
- What is the significance of reading this passage as a dramatic confrontation between two different kingdoms, with two very different kings? How might seeing the passage in this way affect your personal allegiances and those of your faith community?

PRAY

God, all-powerful, most holy sublime ruler of all, you alone are good—supremely, fully, completely good; may we render to you all praise, all honor, and all blessing. May we always ascribe to you alone everything that is good. Amen.

—Francis of Assisi (thirteenth century)

EXPLORE

Wright, N. T. *How God Became King: The Forgotten Story of the Gospels.* New York: HarperCollins, 2012.

5

Why Sabbath?

WHY DO WE OBSERVE SABBATH? Many of us are familiar with the Exodus version of the sabbath command, referencing God's rest on the seventh day of creation. But, what do we find as being the immediate rationale for sabbath as explained in the book of Deuteronomy?

> *Observe the Sabbath day by keeping it holy, as the Lord your God has commanded you. Six days you shall labor and do all your work, but the seventh day is a sabbath to the Lord your God. On it you shall not do any work, neither you, nor your son or daughter, nor your male or female servant, nor your ox, your donkey or any of your animals, nor any foreigner residing in your towns, so that your male and female servants may rest, as you do. Remember that you were slaves in Egypt and that the Lord your God brought you out of there with a mighty hand and an outstretched arm. Therefore the Lord your God has commanded you to observe the Sabbath day.*
> —DEUTERONOMY 5:12–15 (NIV)

So, why sabbath? And what, as presented in the book of Deuteronomy, does it mean to keep it holy? At its most basic, sabbath exists because the Hebrews had now been set free. No longer were they slaves, beasts of burden valued merely for their capacity to produce. Moreover, Deuteronomy tells us, "You must purge the evil [of slavery] from among you."[1] Sabbath exists therefore as an unabashed affirmation of the dignity of the human person. In direct defiance of our most basic economic presuppositions, sabbath forces us to reexamine those unjust practices upon which so much of our

---

1. Deuteronomy 24:7 (NIV)

consumerist culture and so many of our contemporary conveniences are built. It's about embracing our God-given value over and above our market value and weekly rediscovering our essential humanity.

Likewise, sabbath forces us to ask critical questions with regard to the well-being of our global neighbors. We must examine, for instance, issues of fair-trade agriculture, supply chain justice for raw materials (e.g., silicon or cobalt), living wages for blue-collar workers, retail scheduling practices designed to deny full-time benefits, contract labor as a means of sidestepping labor laws, our treatment of and respect for "essential workers" during a global pandemic, and much more. It is for reasons such as this that Christ would one day declare, in the face of an ultimately dehumanizing and oppressive religious culture, that "the sabbath was made for humankind, not humankind for the sabbath."[2] I think it is therefore fair to assert based upon today's reading that "the economy was made for humankind, not humankind for the economy!"

REFLECT

- How have you or your faith community understood the meaning and practice of sabbath?
- What are the possible socio-cultural implications, if any, of a renewed pursuit of sabbath as seen through the lens of human dignity?

PRAY

> We invoke your grace and wisdom, O Lord, upon all people of good will who employ and control the labor of others. Amid the numberless irritations and anxieties of their position, help them to keep a quiet and patient temper, and to rule firmly and wisely, without harshness and anger. Since they hold power over the bread, the safety, and the hopes of the workers, may they wield their powers justly and with love, as older siblings and leaders in the great fellowship of labor. Suffer not the heavenly light of compassion for the weak and the old to be quenched in their hearts. When they are tempted to follow the ruthless ways of others, and to sacrifice human health and life for profit, do strengthen their will in the hour of need, and bring to naught the counsels of the heartless. Save them from repressing their workers into sullen submission and helpless fear.

---

2. Mark 2:27 (NRSV)

Why Sabbath?

May they not sin against Christ by using the bodies and souls of men and women as mere tools to make things, forgetting the human hearts and longings of these their siblings. Raise up among us employers who shall be makers of people as well as of goods. Give us masters in industry who will use their higher ability and knowledge in lifting the workers to increasing independence and vigor, and who will train their helpers for the larger responsibilities of the coming age. Give us men and women of faith who will see beyond the strife of the present and catch a vision of a nobler organization of our work, when all will still follow the leadership of the ablest, not in fear but by the glad will of all, and when none shall be master and none shall be man or woman, but all shall stand side by side in a strong and righteous siblinghood of work.

—Walter Rauschenbusch (1910)

EXPLORE

Kaemingk, Matthew, and Cory B. Willson. *Work and Worship: Reconnecting Our Labor and Liturgy*. Grand Rapids: Baker Academic, 2020.

Stearns, Richard. *The Hole in Our Gospel: What Does God Expect of Us? The Answer that Changed My Life and Might Just Change the World*. Tenth Anniversary Edition. Nashville: Thomas Nelson, 2019.

6

The Stranger

THE TOPIC OF "ALIENS AND strangers" residing among us—migrants, refugees, foreigners, non-citizens, outcasts, or even enemies—looms large throughout Scripture, not to mention contemporary headlines and increasingly xenophobic discourses the world over. According to a 2019 study by the United Nations Department of Economic and Social Affairs, 3.5 percent of the global population, representing approximately 272 million people, are migrants.[1] And the number only increases when considering internally displaced persons. In fact, many of us are or have been migrants ourselves. Be it voluntary or involuntary, for economic opportunity on the one hand or forced displacement on the other, migration and the myriad responses to it are among the greatest issues facing our world today. So, when it comes to our respect for and treatment of the "stranger in our midst," the following verses are but a sampling of the many responsibilities placed upon us by Scripture:

> *When a foreigner resides among you in your land, do not mistreat them. The foreigner residing among you must be treated as your native-born. Love them as yourself, for you were foreigners in Egypt. I am the Lord your God.*
>
> —LEVITICUS 19:33–34 (NIV)

> *The Lord watches over the strangers; he upholds the orphan and the widow, but the way of the wicked he brings to ruin.*
>
> —PSALM 146:9 (NRSV)

---

1. UN DESA, *Migration* 2019, iv–v.

The Stranger

I was hungry and you gave me food, I was thirsty and you gave me drink, I was a stranger and you welcomed me.
—Matthew 25:35 (NRSV)

Keep on loving one another as brothers and sisters. Do not forget to show hospitality to strangers, for by so doing some people have shown hospitality to angels without knowing it. Continue to remember those in prison as if you were together with them in prison, and those who are mistreated as if you yourselves were suffering.
—Hebrews 13:1–3 (NIV)

Whether in America (where I am from) or the Middle East (where I once lived), I have seen firsthand the revolutionary power of intentional, sacrificial hospitality. Through the course of what World Vision President Emeritus Richard Stearns described as "the worst humanitarian crisis of our time,"[2] I witnessed churches in Lebanon undertake the emotionally difficult decision to welcome Syrian refugees within their respective communities. Remarkably, many of these Lebanese had suffered considerably under the past twenty-nine-year military occupation of their country by Syria. While I do not wish to paint an overly positive picture, I witnessed lives and communities transformed in response.

Unfortunately, I have also observed the oftentimes tragic, violent, and exploitative consequences of exclusion as too many refugees and migrants suffer the consequences of forced confinement, sterilization, child separation, statelessness, scapegoating, and life in multi-generation refugee camps—all without recourse to legal rights or protection and accompanied by a profusion of physical, emotional, sexual, economic, and even spiritual exploitation. In the worst-case scenarios, refugees, migrants, and especially the "indigenous other" (think: Native Americans, European Jews, Muslims in India, China, and Myanmar, Palestinians, black South Africans, Rwandan Tutsi, and far too many others) have been subject to horrifying pogroms of ethnic cleansing and genocide.

REFLECT

- In your context, who has been considered an alien or stranger? What about the indigenous other? To what extent are such persons accepted and loved or a source of resentment and mistrust within your community?

2. Stearns, quoted in Kashouh, *Turbulent Times*, i.

- What would a commitment to intentional hospitality look like within your community or nation?

PRAY

> *O God, you made us in your own image and redeemed us through Jesus your son: Look with compassion on the whole human family; take away the arrogance and hatred which infect our hearts; break down the walls that separate us; unite us in bonds of love; and work through our struggle and confusion to accomplish your purposes on earth; that, in your good time, all nations and races may serve you in harmony around your heavenly throne; through Jesus Christ our Lord. Amen.*
>
> —The Book of Common Prayer (1979)

EXPLORE

Das, Rupen, and Brent Hamoud. *Strangers in the Kingdom: Ministering to Refugees, Migrants and the Stateless.* Carlisle: Langham Global Library, 2017.

Kashouh, Hikmat. *Following Jesus in Turbulent Times: Disciple-Making in the Arab World.* Carlisle: Langham Global Library, 2018.

Migration Data Portal (migrationdataportal.org).

7

Every Tear

OF PARAMOUNT IMPORTANCE TO THE socio-political outlook of our Christian faith is the final, culminating vision of Scripture—when the work first begun in Christ and taken up by his followers finds its ultimate fulfillment—because our beliefs about the future give shape to our interpretation of contemporary events and motivate our present courses of action:

> *And there were loud voices in heaven, which said: "The kingdom of the world has become the kingdom of our Lord and of his Messiah, and he will reign for ever and ever."*
> —REVELATION 11:15 (NIV)

> *Then I saw "a new heaven and a new earth," for the first heaven and the first earth had passed away, and there was no longer any sea. I saw the Holy City, the new Jerusalem, coming down out of heaven from God, prepared as a bride beautifully dressed for her husband.*
>
> *And I heard a loud voice from the throne saying, "Look! God's dwelling place is now among the people, and he will dwell with them. They will be his people and God himself will be their God. 'He will wipe every tear from their eyes. There will be no more death' or mourning or crying or pain, for the old order of things has passed away."*
>
> *He who was seated on the throne said, "I am making everything new!" Then he said, "Write this down, for these words are trustworthy and true."*
>
> *He said to me: "It is done. I am the Alpha and the Omega, the Beginning and the End. To the thirsty I will give water without cost*

from the spring of the water of life. Those who are victorious will inherit all this, and I will be their God and they will be my children.

—REVELATION 21:1–7 (NIV)

We are presented neither with an escapist image of a far-off heaven nor of apocalyptic destruction. Rather, the passage describes a future, material vision of complete and total transformation, not universal devastation! It is a vision of a world without evil, of God taking up residence to dwell among his people, of the full and final reunification of heaven and earth. In the words of New Testament scholar Michael J. Gorman,

> This vision—or, rather, this oncoming reality—is the *climax of the book of Revelation, the New Testament, and the entire Bible, the whole story of God, and also the story of humanity.* As such, it is aesthetically, literally, and theologically satisfying. The vision of a 'new heaven and new earth' does not mean the destruction and replacement of the material world but its transformation, especially the transformation of human existence within that material world. The culture of the beast has been replaced by the culture of the Lamb; a culture of death by a culture of life; a culture of insecurity and fear by a culture of peace and trust. The new heaven, new earth, and new city are not, therefore, some kind of ethereal mist, but very real. This eschatological reality is not an escape from the materiality of existence but the very fulfillment of material existence . . . Paradise, the original creation depicted in Genesis, has been restored, not abandoned or destroyed.[1]

It is this future vision which gives shape to our present task as followers of Jesus Christ.

REFLECT

- How have you or your faith community understood the return of Christ and the fate of the material world?

- If we accept that our beliefs about the future give shape to our actions in the present, then what might be the implications of envisioning the future as the reunification and renewal of heaven and earth—as opposed to a future wherein the souls of the saved depart skyward and away from a planet facing imminent demise?

---

1. Gorman, *Reading Revelation*, Chap. 9.

PRAY

Christ Jesus, we long for the day when the violent, oppressive, and broken kingdoms of this world become the kingdom of the Lord, when all has been made new, and we experience no longer the trauma of death, or mourning, or crying, or pain. Forgive us those times we have allowed our nightmarish misconceptions about the future to manifest in the lived, present-day nightmares and suffering of your children, our fellow earth-bound brothers and sisters. Empower us by the Holy Spirit to live in hopeful anticipation of your promised future, clinging to it as a guiding light and allowing it to inform and give shape to our contemporary realities. In your holy name we pray, Lord Jesus. Amen.

—A Prayer for the Present (original)

EXPLORE

Gorman, Michael J. *Reading Revelation Responsibly: Uncivil Worship and Witness: Following the Lamb into the New Creation.* Eugene: Cascade, 2011.

Bible Project. "Heaven & Earth." https://bibleproject.com/explore/heaven-earth/.

8

Supremely Good

FROM HISTORY'S END, WE TURN now back to its beginning:

> *Then God said, "Let us make humanity in our image to resemble us so that they may take charge of the fish of the sea, the birds in the sky, the livestock, all the earth, and all the crawling things on earth."*
> *God created humanity in God's own image, in the divine image God created them, male and female God created them. God blessed them and said to them, "Be fertile and multiply; fill the earth and master it. Take charge of the fish of the sea, the birds in the sky, and everything crawling on the ground."*
> *Then God said, "I now give to you all the plants on the earth that yield seeds and all the trees whose fruit produces its seeds within it. These will be your food. To all wildlife, to all the birds in the sky, and to everything crawling on the ground—to everything that breathes— I give all the green grasses for food." And that's what happened.*
> *God saw everything he had made: it was supremely good.*
> —GENESIS 1:26–31 (CEB)

There is so much within this passage to unpack, but to venture a start:

1. Creation—the material world—is fundamentally good, crafted with purpose, intentionality, and great care. As such, the first chapter of Genesis represents an intentional polemic against those contemporaneous Near Eastern creation myths within which both material creation and humankind are but afterthoughts to a pantheon of capricious, self-serving, and war-like deities.

2. Each of us was made in the very image of God. The pagan gods had statues; God has us. And upon this truth is based the inherent dignity and worth and therefore inalienable rights of *all* persons.
3. Being made in his image, God has entrusted us with the wise management, the care and stewardship—not rapacious exploitation!—of his world. Creation care can in many respects be seen as our very first commandment.
4. Within this passage is also found the basis for the fundamental equality of women and men, a truth built into the very fabric of creation and intrinsic to God's very image. And, it is a truth with ramifications for all domains of life.
5. Finally, the theological depth and message of this passage far surpasses and makes largely irrelevant any attempt to use it as ammunition in modern debates regarding faith and science.

REFLECT

- Do any of the five points above apply specifically to a situation you are facing? How does the Genesis account assist you in thinking about that specific situation?
- Within your own faith community or socio-political context, how might the theological message of this passage lead to a renewed emphasis on any one of the following: human dignity, creation care, gender equality, or the validity of science. Choose one to consider prayerfully.

PRAY

> *O God, we thank you for this universe, our great home; for its vastness and its riches, and for the manifoldness of the life which teems upon it and of which we are part. We praise you for the arching sky and the blessed winds, for the driving clouds and the constellations on high. We praise you for the salt sea and the running water, for the everlasting hills, for the trees, and for the grass under our feet. We thank you for our senses by which we can see the splendor of the morning, hear the jubilant songs of love, and smell the breath of the springtime. Grant us, we pray, a heart wide open to all this joy and beauty. Save our souls from being so steeped in care or so darkened*

by passion that we pass heedless and unseeing when even the thorn bush by the wayside is aflame with the glory of God.

Enlarge within us the sense of fellowship with all living things, our little brothers and sisters, to whom you have given this earth as their home in common with us. We remember with shame that in the past we have exercised the high dominion of humankind with ruthless cruelty, so that the voice of the earth, which should have gone up to you in song, has been a groan of travail. May we realize that they live, not for us alone, but for themselves and for you, and that they love the sweetness of life even as we, and serve you in their place better than we in ours. When our use of this world is over and we make room for others, may we not leave anything ravished by our greed or spoiled by our ignorance; but may we hand on our common heritage fairer and sweeter through our use of it, undiminished in fertility and joy, that so our bodies may return in peace to the [earth that] nourished them and our spirits may round the circle of a perfect life in you. Amen.

—Walter Rauschenbusch (1910)

EXPLORE

Sarna, Nahum. *Understanding Genesis*. New York: Jewish Theological Seminary, 1966.
Walton, John H. *The Lost World of Genesis One: Ancient Cosmology and the Origins Debate*. Downers Grove: IVP Academic, 2010.

9

Religion: Pure & Faultless

A CONSISTENT THEME THROUGHOUT SCRIPTURE is that, along with the migrant, God stands on the side of the widow and orphan:

> *Do not deprive the foreigner or the fatherless of justice, or take the cloak of the widow as a pledge. Remember that you were slaves in Egypt and the Lord your God redeemed you from there. That is why I command you to do this.*
>
> *When you are harvesting in your field and you overlook a sheaf, do not go back to get it. Leave it for the foreigner, the fatherless and the widow, so that the Lord your God may bless you in all the work of your hands. When you beat the olives from your trees, do not go over the branches a second time. Leave what remains for the foreigner, the fatherless and the widow. When you harvest the grapes in your vineyard, do not go over the vines again. Leave what remains for the foreigner, the fatherless and the widow. Remember that you were slaves in Egypt. That is why I command you to do this.*
>
> —DEUTERONOMY 24:17–22 (NIV)

> *Learn to do right! Seek justice, encourage the oppressed. Defend the cause of the fatherless, plead the case of the widow.*
>
> —ISAIAH 1:17 (NIV)

> *Religion that God our Father accepts as pure and faultless is this: to look after orphans and widows in their distress and to keep oneself from being polluted by the world. My brothers and sisters, believers in our glorious Lord Jesus Christ must not show favoritism.*
>
> —JAMES 1:27 (NIV)

Within the deeply patriarchal, tribal context of the ancient near east, God stands with society's most vulnerable—those lacking social capital, most subject to the vicissitudes of the powerful or the callousness of impersonal economic forces. In keeping with the socio-economic realities of the era, widows, orphans, and migrants were particularly vulnerable and, as such, became emblematic of those persons most in need of support by the community of faith. Likewise, if we are to live in faithful obedience to the word of God, then our contemporary communities must guarantee the existence of legal, financial, and socio-political safeguards for those lacking recourse to standard means of support. We must never allow anyone to fall through the cracks. For a society is not judged by God on the value of its stock market or the strength of its middle class, but by the health and well-being of its most vulnerable—a situation akin to Pedro Arrupe and Paul VI's declaration that the church acts with a "preferential respect," or "option," for the poor.[1] As Daniel Groody writes, "The single most important criterion of the health of a society is how it treats its most vulnerable members and how it responds to the needs of the poor through its public policies."[2] If only our contemporary political-economic discourses reflected such a concern.

REFLECT

- To what extent has the well-being of society's most vulnerable been prioritized by your own faith community?
- Think of two practical steps to support the vulnerable members of your community that you can then bring before your local leadership for discussion and planning.

PRAY

> *Lord God, graciously comfort and care for all who are imprisoned, hungry, thirsty, naked and miserable; also all widows, orphans, sick, and sorrowing. In brief, give us our daily bread, so that Christ may abide in us and we in him forever, and that with him we may worthily bear the name of Christian.*
>
> —MARTIN LUTHER (SIXTEENTH CENTURY)

---

1. Arrupe, "Poverty," §1; Paul VI, *Octogesima Adveniens*, §23.
2. Groody, *Globalization*, Chap. 4.

EXPLORE

Câmara, Hélder. *Dom Hélder Câmara: Essential Writings.* Edited by Francis McDonagh. Maryknoll: Orbis, 2009.

Groody, Daniel G. *Globalization, Spirituality, and Justice: Navigating a Path to Peace.* Revised Edition. Maryknoll: Orbis, 2015.

10

Kingdom Economics 101

WHILE SPEAKING TO THE OVERWHELMING grace of God, the following parable offers a pointed critique of our most basic economic assumptions. Jesus reminds us that human value must always supersede market value. It's Kingdom Economics 101.

> *For the kingdom of heaven is like a landowner who went out early in the morning to hire workers for his vineyard. He agreed to pay them a denarius* [a fair, living wage] *for the day and sent them into his vineyard.*
>
> *About nine in the morning he went out and saw others standing in the marketplace doing nothing. He told them, "You also go and work in my vineyard, and I will pay you whatever is right." So they went.*
>
> *He went out again about noon and about three in the afternoon and did the same thing. About five in the afternoon he went out and found still others standing around. He asked them, "Why have you been standing here all day long doing nothing?"*
>
> *"Because no one has hired us," they answered.*
>
> *He said to them, "You also go and work in my vineyard."*
>
> *When evening came, the owner of the vineyard said to his foreman, "Call the workers and pay them their wages, beginning with the last ones hired and going on to the first."*
>
> *The workers who were hired about five in the afternoon came and each received a denarius. So when those came who were hired first, they expected to receive more. But each one of them also received a denarius. When they received it, they began to grumble against the landowner. "These who were hired last worked only one*

hour," they said, "and you have made them equal to us who have borne the burden of the work and the heat of the day."

But he answered one of them, "I am not being unfair to you, friend. Didn't you agree to work for a denarius? Take your pay and go. I want to give the one who was hired last the same as I gave you. Don't I have the right to do what I want with my own money? Or are you envious because I am generous?"

So the last will be first, and the first will be last.

—MATTHEW 20:1–16 (NIV)

Do not take advantage of a hired worker who is poor and needy, whether that worker is a fellow Israelite or a foreigner residing in one of your towns. Pay them their wages each day before sunset, because they are poor and are counting on it. Otherwise they may cry to the Lord against you, and you will be guilty of sin.

—DEUTERONOMY 24:14–15 (NIV)

As we place ourselves in the position of day laborer, gig worker, or independent contractor—positions familiar perhaps to many of us—Christ's parable forces us to revisit questions related to living wages, universal basic income, and the right to dignity in work. Likewise, it challenges the widespread, but nevertheless false assumption that our profession or economic situation would somehow make us more or less deserving of life's basic necessities than another. Economic productivity is an inadequate arbiter of value. So, each laborer deserves a living wage regardless of employment status. As New Testament scholar Kenneth E. Bailey writes, "Justice is more than the equal application of law. In this parable, justice includes respect for the dignity of those in need and a deep concern for their welfare." To which he adds, "The parable offers an example of an employer who has compassion for the unemployed and who shows amazing sensitivity to both their physical needs and self-respect."[1] Such is the heart of God.

REFLECT

- In what ways might the actions of the compassionate employer challenge not only our basic economic assumptions but also, like those who had worked all day, our instinctive sense of fairness?

---

1. Bailey, *Middle Eastern Eyes*, 363.

- How might the lessons of the parable of the compassionate employer be implemented within your own community or wider socio-economic context?

PRAY

> *Heavenly Father, we remember before you those who suffer want and anxiety from lack of work. Guide the people of this land so to use our public and private wealth that all may find suitable and fulfilling employment, and receive just payment for their labor; through Jesus Christ our Lord. Amen.*
>
> —The Book of Common Prayer (1979)

EXPLORE

Bailey, Kenneth E. *Jesus through Middle Eastern Eyes: Cultural Studies in the Gospels.* Downers Grove: IVP Academic, 2009.

11

Kingdom Economics 102

ECHOING DEUTERONOMY, THE FOLLOWING PARABLE of Jesus takes aim once again at our implicit socio-economic assumptions. We can consider this Kingdom Economics 102.

> When you are harvesting in your field and you overlook a sheaf, do not go back to get it. Leave it for the foreigner, the fatherless and the widow, so that the Lord your God may bless you in all the work of your hands.
> —DEUTERONOMY 24:19 (NIV)

> Someone in the crowd said to him, "Teacher, tell my brother to divide the inheritance with me."
> Jesus replied, "Man, who appointed me a judge or an arbiter between you?" Then he said to them, "Watch out! Be on your guard against all kinds of greed; life does not consist in an abundance of possessions."
> And he told them this parable: "The ground of a certain rich man yielded an abundant harvest. He thought to himself, 'What shall I do? I have no place to store my crops.'
> "Then he said, 'This is what I'll do. I will tear down my barns and build bigger ones, and there I will store my surplus grain.' And I'll say to myself, 'You have plenty of grain laid up for many years. Take life easy; eat, drink and be merry.'
> "But God said to him, 'You fool! This very night your life will be demanded from you. Then who will get what you have prepared for yourself?'"

> "This is how it will be with whoever stores up things for themselves but is not rich toward God."
>
> —LUKE 12:15–21 (NIV)

Luke's first-century readers would have immediately recognized that the rich fool rebuilt his barns in direct defiance of an explicit, oft-repeated scriptural mandate to leave the excess of one's produce for the poor, the alien, the orphan, and the widow—society's most vulnerable. For this reason, Ambrose of Milan of the fourth century proclaimed,

> It is not from your own possessions that you are bestowing alms on the poor; you are but restoring to them what is theirs by right. For what was given to everyone for the use of all, you have taken for your exclusive use. The earth belongs not to the rich, but to everyone. Thus, far from giving lavishly, you are but paying part of your debt.[1]

In his abundance, the rich fool forgot that all things, including life itself, were not his to possess but merely on loan from God for the benefit of all. As Ambrose's celebrated disciple, Augustine of Hippo, would later declare, "He did not realize that the bellies of the poor were much safer storerooms than his barns."[2]

REFLECT

- What exactly was so objectionable regarding the actions of the rich fool?
- Consider one specific application of this parable for the socio-economic life of your community or wider social context?

PRAY

> Lord, I commit my failures as well as my successes into your hands, and I bring for your healing the people and the situations, the wrongs and the hurts of the past. Give me courage, strength and generosity to let go and move on, leaving the past behind me, and living the present to the full. Lead me always to be positive as I entrust the past to your mercy, the present to your love, and the future to your providence.
>
> —AUGUSTINE OF HIPPO (FOURTH CENTURY)

1. Ambrose, quoted in Paul VI, *Populorum Progressio*, §23.
2. Augustine, quoted in Bailey, *Middle Eastern Eyes*, 304.

EXPLORE

Das, Rupen. *Compassion and the Mission of God: Revealing the Invisible Kingdom.* Carlisle: Langham Global Library, 2016.

12

Joy, Justice, & Peace

RETURNING FROM THE WILDERNESS, JESUS inaugurated his public ministry with the following vision of Isaiah in a passage encapsulating his kingdom mission and message:

> *The people walking in darkness have seen a great light; on those living in the land of deep darkness a light has dawned* [Glory].
>
> *You have enlarged the nation and increased their joy; they rejoice before you as people rejoice at the harvest, as warriors rejoice when dividing the plunder* [Joy].
>
> *For as in the day of Midian's defeat, you have shattered the yoke that burdens them, the bar across their shoulders, the rod of their oppressor* [Justice].
>
> *Every warrior's boot used in battle and every garment rolled in blood will be destined for burning, will be fuel for the fire* [Peace].
>
> *For to us a child is born, to us a son is given, and the government will be on his shoulders. And he will be called Wonderful Counselor, Mighty God, Everlasting Father, Prince of Peace.*
>
> *Of the greatness of his government and peace there will be no end. He will reign on David's throne and over his kingdom, establishing and upholding it with justice and righteousness from that time on and forever. The zeal of the Lord Almighty will accomplish this.*
>
> —ISAIAH 9:2–7 (NIV)

Leaving Nazareth, [Jesus] went and lived in Capernaum, which was by the lake in the area of Zebulun and Naphtali—to fulfill what was said through the prophet Isaiah: "Land of Zebulun and land of Naphtali, the Way of the Sea, beyond the Jordan, Galilee of the

Joy, Justice, & Peace

> *Gentiles—the people living in darkness have seen a great light; on those living in the land of the shadow of death a light has dawned."*
>
> *From that time on Jesus began to preach, "Repent, for the kingdom of heaven has come near."*
>
> —Matthew 4:13–17 (NIV)

"Modern scholarship," writes New Testament scholar George Eldon Ladd, "is quite unanimous in the opinion that the kingdom of God was the central message of Jesus."[1] What, however, are the marks or characteristics of the messianic kingdom? Utilizing imagery from the ancient Near East, the prophet envisions a future kingdom defined in its essence by joy, justice, peace, and the glory, or presence, of God. This is the kingdom announced by Jesus and the lens through which we must view his earthly ministry. As citizens of God's kingdom, this is likewise the vision towards which followers of Christ presently struggle (though it ultimately remains the mission of the Holy Spirit alongside whom we are invited to participate). We strive to see this future vision become a present-day reality, seeking to manifest the joy, justice, and peace of God's glorious kingdom on earth as it is in heaven. However, it is worth asking the activists among us how often joy is seen as a requisite component to our pursuit of justice and peace? Do we view this work as central to the mission of the Spirit's presence in our midst, and do we see the Spirit's presence as integral to our work?

REFLECT

- To what extent does your spiritual and moral life rest upon experiencing the joy of God's presence as much as it does the pursuit of justice and peace?
- Envision within your context a society marked by joy, justice, peace, and the glory of God. What does such a community look like, and what proactive steps might be taken in response to this vision?

PRAY

> *May every breath be for you; may every minute be spent for you. Help us to live while we live, and while we are busy in the world as we must be, for we are called to it, may we sanctify the world for your service. May we be lumps of salt in the midst of society. May our spirit and temper as well as our conversation be heavenly. May*

---

1. Ladd, *Theology*, 54.

there be an influence about us that shall make the world the better before we leave it. Lord, hear us in this thing.

And now that we have your ear, we would pray for this poor world in which we live. We are often horrified by it. O, Lord, we wish that we did not know anything about it for our own comfort. We have said, "Oh! for a lodge in some vast wilderness." We hear of oppression and robbery and murder, and men seem let loose against each other. Lord, have mercy upon this great and wicked city. What is to be done with these millions? What can we do? At least help every child of yours to do his or her utmost. May none of us contribute to the evil directly or indirectly, but may we contribute to the good that is in it.

—Charles Spurgeon (nineteenth century)

EXPLORE

Ladd, George Eldon, and Donald A. Hagner. *A Theology of the New Testament*. Revised Edition. Grand Rapids: Eerdmans, 2010.

13

Seek the Peace

IN HIS LETTER TO THE Judean captives exiled in Babylon, the prophet Jeremiah proclaims the following message from the Lord:

> *This is what the Lord Almighty, the God of Israel, says to all those I carried into exile from Jerusalem to Babylon:* "Build houses and settle down; plant gardens and eat what they produce. Marry and have sons and daughters; find wives for your sons and give your daughters in marriage, so that they too may have sons and daughters. Increase in number there; do not decrease. Also, seek the peace and prosperity of the city to which I have carried you into exile. Pray to the Lord for it, because if it prospers, you too will prosper."
>
> *Yes, this is what the Lord Almighty, the God of Israel, says:* "Do not let the prophets and diviners among you deceive you. Do not listen to the dreams you encourage them to have. They are prophesying lies to you in my name. I have not sent them," declares the Lord.
>
> —JEREMIAH 29:4–9 (NIV)

A very strong case can be made that the books of the Bible, Old and New Testament alike, comprise an extended argument as to what faithfulness to God looks like in the midst of exile for those having lost temple, land, and power. The theme of exile runs through the entirety of Scripture, starting with the primordial exile of our spiritual ancestors Adam and Eve from the garden of Eden. Abraham, likewise, is a sojourner in foreign land, as are Jacob and the twelve tribes of Israel. In their writings, the biblical historians and prophets focus on the significance of events leading up to, during, and immediately following the Babylonian captivity. Finally, the theme of exile is consolidated in the New Testament upon the life, death, and resurrection of Jesus, an event foreshadowing the destruction of the second temple and later all Judea by Rome. (Rabbinic Judaism would develop also in response to this destruction.)

As citizens of a kingdom not from this world (as "resident aliens") our task as the people of God is to strive for the peace and prosperity of the land in which God has placed us, recognizing in the midst of it that God remains with us in our exile. In this way, exile becomes the catalyst for our mission to the world. Meanwhile, those false prophets fabricating promises of "imminent return and easy victory" over our enemies must not be heeded. For such posturing, often accompanied by violent claims to land, power, and religio-cultural supremacy, is simply a misguided attempt to force God's hand. And, it is a terrible witness to the crucified Christ.

REFLECT

- If we are "exiles," why does the prophet command us to "seek the peace and prosperity of the city" in which God has placed us?
- If we truly think of ourselves as exiles, what implications does that have for our earthly allegiances (e.g., nation, church, race, religion, family, tribe, etc.)? How might thinking of ourselves as exiles help us comprehend our own situations of displacement and loss?

PRAY

Lord, make me an instrument of your peace. Where there is hatred, let me sow love; where there is injury, pardon; where there is doubt, faith; where there is despair, hope; where there is darkness, light; where there is sadness, joy. O Divine Master, grant that I may not so much seek to be consoled, as to console; to be understood, as to understand; to be loved, as to love with all my soul. For it is in giving that we receive; it is in pardoning that we are pardoned; and it is in dying that we are born to eternal life. Amen.

—Francis of Assisi (thirteenth century)

EXPLORE

Chapman, Colin. *Whose Holy City? Jerusalem and the Future of Peace in the Middle East.* Grand Rapids: Baker, 2004.

Hauerwas, Stanley, and William H. Willimon. *Resident Aliens: Life in the Christian Colony.* Expanded 25th Anniversary Edition. Nashville: Abingdon Press, 2014.

14

The Peacemakers

As followers of the Prince of Peace, it is only natural that we follow his words and therefore commit ourselves to the pursuit of reconciliation and peace.

> *Blessed are the peacemakers, for they will be called children of God.*
> —Matthew 5:9 (NIV)

> *You have heard that it was said to those who lived long ago, "Don't commit murder," and all who commit murder will be in danger of judgment. But I say to you that everyone who is angry with their brother or sister will be in danger of judgment. If they say to their brother or sister, "You idiot," they will be in danger of being condemned by the governing council. And if they say, "You fool," they will be in danger of fiery hell.*
> *Therefore, if you bring your gift to the altar and there remember that your brother or sister has something against you, leave your gift at the altar and go. First make things right with your brother or sister and then come back and offer your gift. Be sure to make friends quickly with your opponents while you are with them on the way to court.*
> —Matthew 5:21–25 (CEB)

It is important to note that this passage is not an impossible prohibition on anger so much as it is a warning against following down the path that leads to hatred and violence. Echoing the late Glen Stassen, it is essential to not misread the teachings of Jesus as a series of near impossible ideals, attainable only in the hereafter, or as a mirror upon which we find reflected our sinful inadequacy in light of the righteousness of God. Instead, Jesus instructs us to remain proactive in our pursuit of reconciliation, as a means of escaping the vicious cycles of hate, violence, and vengeance within which we too often find ourselves trapped: "Go, be reconciled!" Jesus teaches us. Properly understood, the laws of King Jesus are themselves a grace from God, a means of undoing those sinful patterns that contribute to the experience for far too many of hell on earth. They are a means of manifesting and embodying God's just reign, on earth as it is in heaven. In fact, the pursuit of reconciliation is so important that we are actually commanded to seek peace before returning to God in worship.

REFLECT

- What is the connection between being a peacemaker and being called a child of God? Why does Jesus instruct us to pursue reconciliation with our estranged brothers and sisters before returning to God in worship?
- With whom in your community should you pursue reconciliation? What practical steps can you take today?

PRAY

O God, who is the unsearchable abyss of peace, the ineffable sea of love, the fountain of blessings, and the bestower of affection, who sends peace to those that receive it; open to us this day the sea of your love, and water us with the plenteous streams from the riches of your grace. Make us children of quietness, and heirs of peace. Kindle in us the fire of your love; sow in us your fear; strengthen our weakness by your power; bind us closely to you and to each other in one firm bond of unity; for the sake of Jesus Christ. Amen.

—SYRIAN CLEMENTINE LITURGY (THIRD CENTURY)

EXPLORE

Stassen, Glen H. *Living the Sermon on the Mount: A Practical Hope for Grace and Deliverance.* San Francisco: Jossey-Bass, 2006.

15

Even the Gentiles

TODAY, WE CONTINUE IN THE truth that to follow the Prince of Peace is to follow his specific teachings as recorded in the gospels, popularly referred to as "the red letters," and commit ourselves to the pursuit of peace and reconciliation.

> *You have heard that it was said, "You must love your neighbor and hate your enemy." But I say to you, love your enemies and pray for those who harass you so that you will be acting as children of your Father who is in heaven. He makes the sun rise on both the evil and the good and sends rain on both the righteous and the unrighteous. If you love only those who love you, what reward do you have? Don't even the tax collectors do the same? And if you greet only your brothers and sisters, what more are you doing? Don't even the Gentiles do the same? Therefore, just as your heavenly Father is complete in showing love to everyone, so also you must be complete.*
>
> —MATTHEW 5:43–48 (CEB)

It must be remembered just how easy it is for us to love our "neighbors" while hating our "enemies." This is the essence of partisan polarization in America, religious sectarianism in the Middle East or South Asia, ethnonationalist violence in Europe, and tribal conflict in Africa. It's as natural to us as breathing and has served as a justification for violent conflict the world over. The truth, however, runs deeper than simple-minded hatred. For our fundamental conceptions of history, morality, and even reality itself are very much the byproducts of our socio-cultural allegiances. Situations of conflict call each of these into question and often prove destabilizing to our most basic sense of self, purpose, and belonging. But, to love our "enemy" is to recognize that all are the beloved creations of God and to proactively deconstruct the emotional, psychological, ideological, and quite often physical walls we erect between ourselves and others. Ultimately, that which unites us far outweighs that which tears us apart.

REFLECT

- How many of our stories in literature, cinema, television, and so forth feature a reluctant hero spurred to action only after the tragic loss of a beloved family member or friend? Likewise, how many feature faceless enemies or villains so ruthless and inhuman in their cruelty that any action taken against them is seen as justified? What impact do such stories have on us as a culture?
- Be it personal or political, local or international, who is your "enemy"? What does loving them look like in practice?

PRAY

> *O God, the father of all, whose son commanded us to love our enemies: Lead them and us from prejudice to truth; deliver them and us from hatred, cruelty, and revenge; and in your good time enable us all to stand reconciled before you; through Jesus Christ our Lord. Amen.*
>
> —The Book of Common Prayer (1979)

EXPLORE

Munayer, Salim J., and Lisa Loden. *Through My Enemy's Eyes: Envisioning Reconciliation in Israel-Palestine.* Milton Keynes: Paternoster, 2014.

Volf, Miroslav. *Exclusion and Embrace: A Theological Exploration of Identity, Otherness, and Reconciliation.* Revised and Updated. Nashville: Abingdon Press, 2019.

16

Flipping the Script

LOOKING AGAIN TO THE WORDS of Jesus as presented by Matthew, we can see what a commitment to reconciliation and peace looks like in the face of aggression:

> You know that you have been taught, "An eye for an eye and a tooth for a tooth." But I tell you not to try to get even with a person who has done something to you. When someone slaps your right cheek, turn and let that person slap your other cheek. If someone sues you for your shirt, give up your coat as well. If a soldier forces you to carry his pack one mile, carry it two miles. When people ask you for something, give it to them. When they want to borrow money, lend it to them.
>
> —MATTHEW 5:38–41 (CEV)

First, it must be said that this passage is not an exhortation to passivity in the face of ongoing abuse or structural injustice. God forbid! Rather, when understood through the lens of first-century Palestinian society, daily enduring the violence of Roman military occupation, it becomes a recipe for creative, proactive resistance. It's empowerment by means of sacrificial service and transformative action. It's the way of the cross. As the scholars tell us, to "turn the other cheek" within the honor-bound society of the day is to non-violently force an aggressor to strike you again as equal rather than subordinate.[1] To offer someone your cloak (recalling Deuteronomy 24:10–13) is to stand naked in your generosity before the court, shaming not yourself but your accuser in the process. "Going the extra mile"

---

1. Sennott, *Body and Blood*, 417–418.

references a law allowing centurions to coerce subject persons to travel with them—but only for a single mile! To go a second mile thereby transforms an act of structural humiliation into an act of sacrificial service whilst simultaneously exposing the injustice inherent to the imperial system.[2] In the words of journalist and author Michael Sennott,

> [Jesus] was telling his followers, effectively, "Confront the person offending you, forcing him to face you as an equal, but do not respond with violence in return." That, in the context of Jesus's time and the social and legal codes that existed then, was a radical act of defiance.[3]

These initiatives become a means of flipping the script, of exposing and disrupting imbalances of power without mimicking or reproducing the violence of the aggressor. And in the process, they provoke opportunities for self-reflection, repentance, restitution, and ultimately reconciliation.

REFLECT

- How have you or your community understood the injunctions to "turn the other cheek" and "go the extra mile"? Are there circumstances in which such directives have appeared unrealistic or impractical?
- What might a proactive as opposed to passive understanding of "turning the other cheek" and "going the extra mile" look like practically within your personal and social contexts?

PRAY

> *O God, you have bound us together in a common life. Help us, in the midst of our struggles for justice and truth, to confront one another without hatred or bitterness, and to work together with mutual forbearance and respect; through Jesus Christ our Lord. Amen.*
>
> —THE BOOK OF COMMON PRAYER (1979)

EXPLORE

Buttry, Daniel L. *Peace Warrior: A Memoir from the Front.* Macon: Mercer University Press, 2013.
Sennott, Charles M. *The Body and the Blood: The Middle East's Vanishing Christians and the Possibility for Peace.* New York: Public Affairs, 2002.

2. Stassen and Gushee, *Kingdom Ethics*, 96–98; 314.
3. Sennott, as quoted in Chapman, *Holy City,* 203.

17

Such as These

How often, it must be asked, do we consider the presence and well-being of the children in our midst when organizing or making decisions about our socio-political life?

> People were bringing little children to Jesus for him to place his hands on them, but the disciples rebuked them. When Jesus saw this, he was indignant. He said to them, "Let the little children come to me, and do not hinder them, for the kingdom of God belongs to such as these. Truly I tell you, anyone who will not receive the kingdom of God like a little child will never enter it." And he took the children in his arms, placed his hands on them and blessed them.
>
> —Mark 10:13–16 (NIV)

It's always important to note those moments when Jesus gets angry, for in these moments we find revealed the heart of God. In today's passage, the disciples viewed the children as a peripheral distraction to the mission and message of Christ when in reality they were the central intent. What we learn is that God's in-breaking kingdom belongs not to the prophets, priests, and kings, of whichever era one belongs, but to the children. It might therefore be said that the presence and condition of our children reveals to us the extent to which God's kingdom has been made manifest in our midst—a truth leading Martin Luther, father of the Protestant Reformation, to posit the question, "For what purpose do we older folks exist than to care for, instruct and bring up the young?"[1] To what extent do we

---

1. Quoted in Strohl, "Luther," 134.

consistently act and make decisions with this truth in mind, be it personal or political, inter-communal or economic?

REFLECT

- What impact would it have to make the presence and well-being of children prominent in your personal and communal planning?
- How might church or community activities be organized, or perhaps reorganized, in light of the truth that God's kingdom belongs not to pastors or presidents but children?

PRAY

> *Great father of the weak, lay your hand tenderly on all the little children on earth and bless them. Bless our own children, who are life of our life, and who have become the heart of our heart. Bless every little child-friend that has leaned against our knee and refreshed our soul by its smiling trustfulness. Be good to all children who long in vain for human love, or for flowers and water, and the sweet breast of nature. But bless with a sevenfold blessing the young lives whose slender shoulders are already bowed beneath the yoke of toil, and whose glad growth is being stunted forever... Help us to realize that every child of our nation is in very truth our child, a member of our great family. By the holy child that nestled in Mary's bosom; by the memories of our own childhood joys and sorrows; by the sacred possibilities that slumber in every child, we beseech you to save us from killing the sweetness of young life.*
>
> —WALTER RAUSCHENBUSCH (1910)

EXPLORE

Bunge, Marcia J., ed. *The Child in Christian Thought*. Grand Rapids: Eerdmans, 2001.

18

The One Who Sent Me

TODAY, WE LOOK AGAIN AT the significance of prioritizing the presence and well-being of children as we organize and make decisions about our communal life.

> *They entered Capernaum. When they had come into a house, [Jesus] asked them, "What were you arguing about during the journey?" They didn't respond, since on the way they had been debating with each other about who was the greatest.*
>
> *He sat down, called the Twelve, and said to them, "Whoever wants to be first must be least of all and the servant of all."*
>
> *Jesus reached for a little child, placed him among the Twelve, and embraced him. Then he said, "Whoever welcomes one of these children in my name welcomes me; and whoever welcomes me isn't actually welcoming me but rather the one who sent me."*
>
> —MARK 9:33–37 (CEB)

From the earliest pages of Scripture, children exist as the sign of God's ongoing presence and activity in our midst. As Old Testament scholar Claire R. Matthews McGinnis writes, children represent "the tangible manifestation of God's blessing upon his creation."[1] In the Bible, we find repeated instructions to "be fruitful and multiply," a multiplicity of genealogical lists, and messianic prophecies declaring that "unto us a child is born." We are reminded time and again that God's blessing—his continued care and ultimate plan of salvation for the fallen world—has always gone hand-in-hand with the continued presence and promise of children.

---

1. Matthews McGinnis, "Exodus," 28.

It must be stated, however, that this in no way implies an absence of children as somehow representing the lack of God's blessing or favor, a truth powerfully confirmed by the apostle Paul. But living in community means that we share a collective responsibility for the care and well-being of all our young. For it is not the popes, apostles, patriarchs, or presidents, but the children who represent the sign of God's ongoing presence in our midst. I think it is fair to say therefore that the status of children in our respective societies is emblematic of the status we attribute to God himself. To honor a child is to honor the very presence of God in that child.

REFLECT

- If we associate the presence of children in our community with the presence and activity of God, how does that impact our common life?
- Imagine a community or society that consistently considers the presence, needs, and well-being of its children. With that image in mind, what practical steps might be taken to ensure the well-being of the children within your personal spheres of influence?

PRAY

King Jesus, we love you. Grant us the ability to love others just as you love us so much, and the courage to do for others as we would want them to do for us. Guide and direct us. Help the hungry, sick, and all who are in need. Bless the children of our family, our city, and the world. Surround them with your love, and fill them with your joy that they may grow happy, healthy, and safe for all their lives. In your amazing name we pray, King Jesus. Amen.

—Modified Wheeler Family Prayer (original)

EXPLORE

Bunge, Marcia J., ed. *The Child in the Bible*. Grand Rapids: Eerdmans, 2008.

19

Defacing the Image of God

To emphasize again just how crucial the well-being of our children is to God, I am convinced today's passage is a first-century euphemism for the horrors of child abuse:

> As for whoever causes these little ones who believe in me to trip and fall into sin, it would be better for them to have a huge stone hung around their necks and to be thrown into the lake. If your hand causes you to fall into sin, chop it off. It's better for you to enter into life crippled than to go away with two hands into the fire of hell, which can't be put out. If your foot causes you to fall into sin, chop it off. It's better for you to enter life lame than to be thrown into hell with two feet. If your eye causes you to fall into sin, tear it out. It's better for you to enter God's kingdom with one eye than to be thrown into hell with two.
>
> —Mark 9:42–47 (CEB)

Oftentimes, we are asked to extend grace. This is not one of those times. Anything that prevents a child from experiencing the full fruits of God's kingdom, be it the trauma of poverty, war, exploitation, or abuse, rightly results in his divine wrath. As embodied by the bigoted cruelty of Pharaoh, the infanticidal cult of Moloch, and the paranoid reign of King Herod, the scriptural manifestations of tyrannical, idolatrous evil are those responsible for the slaughter and sacrifice of innocent children—often undertaken in the vain pursuit of power and prosperity. Today, it seems clear to me that we are failing miserably in our collective responsibility as adults, given that millions of children are currently living through the terror of what can only be described as hell on earth:

- in refugee encampments, or migrant detention centers;
- crouched in bomb shelters, fearful of the next barrage;
- in back rooms or back alleys, satisfying the abhorrent desires of wicked men and women;
- in sweltering fields or factories, exploited for their low-cost labor;
- on street corners, begging for their next meal.

If honoring a child is to honor the presence of God in that child, then to harm a child is to deface the very image of God.

REFLECT

- To what extent have we, as a global civilization, abdicated our collective responsibility as adults for the children in our midst?
- What can be done practically to ensure the protection and safety of children in your community? (For instance, do you know of a local refugee assistance or resettlement agency? Does your church or organization have child safety policies in place? Who in your community assists with foster care and adoption? Are there interventions in place for low-performing or at-risk students at school? Are there mechanisms to ensure that all products sold in your area were produced without child labor? And, if such programs and policies do exist in one's community—and many do because they are required by law—are they well-resourced and funded? Are policies enforced? Or are they simply paid lip service to?)

PRAY

Heavenly father, whose unveiled face the angels of little children do always behold, look with love and pity, we beg you, upon the children of our neglect. These children of yours are learning in this school of life the bad lessons of our selfishness and our folly. Save them, and save us, O Lord. Save them from ignorance and brutality, from the shamelessness of lust, the hardness of greed, and the besotting of drink; and save us from the greater guilt of those that offend your little ones, and from the hypocrisy of those that say they see and see not, whose sin remains.

Make clear to those of older years the inalienable right of childhood to play, and give to those who govern our cities the will and ability to provide the places for safety as well as for play; make clear to those who minister to the appetite for recreation the guilt of them that lead children astray; and make clear to us all that the great school of life is not encompassed by walls and that its teachers are all who influence their younger brothers and sisters by companionship and example, whether for good or evil, and that in that school we all are teachers and as we teach we are judged. For all false teaching, for all hindering of your children, pardon us, O Lord, and suffer the little children to come unto you, for Jesus's sake.

—Adapted from Walter Rauschenbusch (1910)

EXPLORE

McConnell, Douglas, Jennifer Orona, and Paul Stockley, eds. *Understanding God's Heart for Children: Toward a Biblical Framework*. Milton Keynes: Authentic Media, 2007.

Wheeler, Jesse Steven. "Defacing the Image of God: The Children of War and Our Collective Human Failure." *The IMES Blog*. Arab Baptist Theological Seminary (2017). IMES.blog.

20

In Their Power

THOUGH FIRST PROCLAIMED MILLENNIA AGO, the following words of the prophet Micah present an accurate depiction of contemporary socio-economic realities:

> *Woe to those who plan iniquity, to those who plot evil on their beds! At morning's light they carry it out because it is in their power to do it. They covet fields and seize them, and houses, and take them. They defraud people of their homes, they rob them of their inheritance.*
>
> —MICAH 2:1–2 (NIV)

> *"Do not prophesy," their prophets say. "Do not prophesy about these things; disgrace will not overtake us."*
>
> —MICAH 2:6 (NIV)

> *You steal the shirts right off the backs of those who trusted you, making them as ragged as men returning from battle. You have evicted women from their pleasant homes and forever stripped their children of all that God would give them.*
>
> —MICAH 2:8–9 (NLT)

> *Suppose a prophet full of lies would say to you, "I'll preach to you the joys of wine and alcohol!" That's just the kind of prophet you would like!*
>
> —MICAH 2:11 (NLT)

The above passage presents us with an image of those in power conspiring to use that power to defraud others of their land, homes, and inheritance: the vulture capitalists of their day and age. It presents us with a social order built upon graft and exploitation in which the system is manipulated, or "rigged," to favor those who use their power to enrich themselves at the expense of others. Finally, it highlights the existence of a false religio-prophetic establishment working to provide ideological cover for the corrupt powers that be. For this reason, Old Testament scholar Walter Brueggemann writes, "It was, in that ancient context, difficult to construe reality outside the blueprints that had been constructed by the powerful."[1]

Far too often in the course of ecclesial history, our leaders and institutions have stood with the status quo and allied themselves with the power brokers of the day. Listening to the prophets, however, and recognizing how often Jesus draws from them in his life and ministry will dispel us of any notion that God stands with the status quo. Our responsibility as followers of Jesus, as those who would stand in the tradition of the biblical prophets, is to speak up and out against any and all forms of exploitation—as well as its ideological enablers—to pursue, in the words of Brueggemann, "an alternative alignment of the political economy."[2]

REFLECT

- What parallels can be drawn between the prophet Micah's ancient near eastern context and the contemporary world of today?
- Are there particular situations of corruption, exploitation, and theft within your context against which you and your faith community can and should speak?

PRAY

> *Look with pity, O heavenly Father, upon the people in this land who live with injustice, terror, disease, and death as their constant companions. Have mercy upon us. Help us to eliminate our cruelty to these our neighbors. Strengthen those who spend their lives establishing equal protection of the law and equal opportunities for all. And grant that every one of us may enjoy a fair portion of the riches of this land; through Jesus Christ our Lord. Amen.*

---

1. Brueggemann, *Judgment to Hope*, 70.
2. Brueggemann, *Judgment to Hope*, 69.

> Serving a Crucified King
>
> —The Book of Common Prayer (1979)

EXPLORE

Brueggemann, Walter. *From Judgment to Hope: A Study on the Prophets.* Louisville: Westminster John Knox Press, 2019.

———. *Interrupting Silence: God's Command to Speak Out.* Louisville: Westminster John Knox Press, 2018.

21

Farmers & Firearms

WITHIN THE FOLLOWING PASSAGE IS found a stunning vision of God's peaceable reign as presented by the prophet Micah:

> *In the last days, the mountain of the Lord's house will be the highest of all—the most important place on earth. It will be raised above the other hills, and people from all over the world will stream there to worship. People from many nations will come and say, "Come, let us go up to the mountain of the Lord, to the house of Jacob's God. There he will teach us his ways, and we will walk in his paths."*
>
> *For the Lord's teaching will go out from Zion; his word will go out from Jerusalem. The Lord will mediate between peoples and will settle disputes between strong nations far away. They will hammer their swords into plowshares and their spears into pruning hooks. Nation will no longer fight against nation, nor train for war anymore. Everyone will live in peace and prosperity, enjoying their own grapevines and fig trees, for there will be nothing to fear.*
>
> —MICAH 4:1–4 (NLT)

A common assertion is that peacebuilding constitutes an unnecessary distraction from the true mission of the church, the evangelistic proclamation of the gospel. Or, if not seen as a distraction, then it is assumed to fall into the category of "nice but ultimately inconsequential." The reign of God, however, is envisioned here by the prophet as an all-encompassing, all-surpassing peace, the reconciliation of all things on earth as it is in heaven. Seen this way, reconciliation between God, self, society, and all creation comprises the very heart of the gospel as Christ proclaimed it. Therefore, to walk in the path of the Lord and know his ways is to devote oneself to the pursuit of peace and reconciliation, to creation and cultivation as opposed to violence and destruction.

Peacebuilding, if understood as the lived pursuit of reconciliation, hardly distracts us from our core vocation as the people of God. It is essential to our very calling. To paraphrase theologians Veli-Matti Kärkkäinen and Amos Yong, this is an honest assessment of the effects of sin upon the whole of life as well as an acknowledgment of the breadth, or "multidimensionality," of salvation.[1] Centered, therefore, on the person, mission, and message of our king and savior Christ Jesus and manifested in his death and resurrection, *reconciliation is the gospel*! As we act in anticipation of the coming kingdom, our mission is to partner with God in doing all we can to see the prophet's future vision become a present-day reality, transforming "swords into plowshares."

REFLECT

- How have you understood the relationship, if any, between peacebuilding and the proclamation of the gospel?
- What practices could your faith community adopt in its pursuit of reconciliation and peace?

PRAY

> *Sovereign and almighty Lord, bless all your people, and all your flock. Give your peace, your help, your love unto us your servants, the sheep of your fold, that we may be united in the bond of peace and love, one body and one spirit, in one hope of our calling, in your divine and boundless love. Amen.*
>
> —From the Alexandrian Liturgy of St. Mark (fourth century)

EXPLORE

Kärkkäinen, Veli-Matti. *Christ and Reconciliation: A Constructive Christian Theology for the Pluralistic World*, vol. 1. Grand Rapids: Eerdmans, 2013.

Wheeler, Jesse Steven. "Kerygmatic Peacebuilding (Part 2): What Does Peace Have to Do with the Gospel?" *The IMES Blog*. Arab Baptist Theological Seminary (2016). IMES. blog.

---

1. Kärkkäinen, *Reconciliation*, 375.

22

What God Wants

THE PROPHET MICAH ASKS WHAT the Lord requires of us:

> *With what shall I come before the Lord, and bow myself before God on high? Shall I come before him with burnt offerings, with calves a year old? Will the Lord be pleased with thousands of rams, with ten thousands of rivers of oil? Shall I give my firstborn for my transgression, the fruit of my body for the sin of my soul?"*
> *He has told you, O mortal, what is good; and what does the Lord require of you but to do justice, and to love kindness, and to walk humbly with your God?*
> —MICAH 6:6–8 (NRSV)

> *What shall I say about the homes of the wicked filled with treasures gained by cheating? What about the disgusting practice of measuring out grain with dishonest measures? How can I tolerate your merchants who use dishonest scales and weights? The rich among you have become wealthy through extortion and violence. Your citizens are so used to lying that their tongues can no longer tell the truth.*
> —MICAH 6:10–12 (NLT)

So much of our religious activity, it could be said, constitutes one giant exercise in missing the point. At times, our misguided religiosity appears relatively benign. At others, it can reach ever-destructive and unimaginable heights in its mistaken pursuit of God's favor. In either case, we are guilty in our self-obsessed worship of trying to love God while simultaneously ignoring the socio-economic exploitation of our neighbors in need. This, the prophet tells us, is an impossibility. In truth, individualized and spiritualized approaches to religion often represent an intentional attempt to divorce faith from its socio-political context, neutering it of its prophetic power and rendering it impotent, even compliant, in the face of the political-economic powers that be. It distracts us from or even serves to justify the exploitation and abuse of others. Yet, what does the Lord require? Justice. Kindness. Mercy. And, humble service: "A readiness," Walter Brueggemann tells us, "to submit one's self willingly to God's purpose for the world."[1]

REFLECT

- Are there times when you have attempted to bargain with God to earn his favor or blessing? Moreover, do you ever find yourself slipping into self-obsessed worship?

- Knowing what the Lord requires of us, what actions might you or your faith community be able to accomplish in your pursuit of justice, kindness, and humble service?

PRAY

> With the psalmist, let us pray the following song to the Lord: *Your unfailing love, O Lord, is as vast as the heavens; your faithfulness reaches beyond the clouds. Your righteousness is like the mighty mountains, your justice like the ocean depths. You care for people and animals alike, O Lord. How precious is your unfailing love, O God! All humanity finds shelter in the shadow of your wings. You feed them from the abundance of your own house, letting them drink from your river of delights. For you are the fountain of life, the light by which we see. Pour out your unfailing love on those who love you; give justice to those with honest hearts. Amen.*
>
> —Psalm 36:5–10 (NLT)

EXPLORE

Gowan, Donald E. *The Theology of the Prophetic Books: The Death & Resurrection of Israel.* Louisville: Westminster John Knox Press, 1998.

---

1. Brueggemann, *Judgment to Hope*, 64.

23

Those on His Right

IN ANY COLLECTION OF PASSAGES focused on faith, politics, and our collective responsibility as followers of Jesus, I would be remiss not to include the following:

> *When the Son of Man comes in his glory, and all the angels with him, he will sit on his glorious throne. All the nations will be gathered before him, and he will separate the people one from another as a shepherd separates the sheep from the goats. He will put the sheep on his right and the goats on his left.*
>
> *Then the King will say to those on his right, "Come, you who are blessed by my Father; take your inheritance, the kingdom prepared for you since the creation of the world. For I was hungry and you gave me something to eat, I was thirsty and you gave me something to drink, I was a stranger and you invited me in, I needed clothes and you clothed me, I was sick and you looked after me, I was in prison and you came to visit me."*
>
> *Then the righteous will answer him, "Lord, when did we see you hungry and feed you, or thirsty and give you something to drink? When did we see you a stranger and invite you in, or needing clothes and clothe you? When did we see you sick or in prison and go to visit you?"*
>
> *The King will reply, "Truly I tell you, whatever you did for one of the least of these brothers and sisters of mine, you did for me."*
>
> *Then he will say to those on his left, "Depart from me, you who are cursed, into the eternal fire prepared for the devil and his angels. For I was hungry and you gave me nothing to eat, I was thirsty and you gave me nothing to drink, I was a stranger and you did not*

invite me in, I needed clothes and you did not clothe me, I was sick and in prison and you did not look after me."

They also will answer, "Lord, when did we see you hungry or thirsty or a stranger or needing clothes or sick or in prison, and did not help you?'

He will reply, "Truly I tell you, whatever you did not do for one of the least of these, you did not do for me"

Then they will go away to eternal punishment, but the righteous to eternal life.

—MATTHEW 25:31–46 (NIV)

REFLECT

Rather than comment on today's passage, I simply ask you to sit with it for a few minutes in silence. Reflect on the magnitude of the scene as presented, on the unmitigated power held in this moment by Christ Jesus over the fate of every living soul. Reflect also upon the criteria he uses to base his decisions. Ask yourself: In whose faces do we find reflected the king of the universe, and do we behave towards such persons in the same manner as we would if standing before Christ on the day of judgement?

PRAY

Then, read the passage again. Focus on the word or phrase that convicts you the most, or upon the section that you find most troubling. Pray over it. Ask the Lord to reveal his heart to you and guide and direct you as to how you might best respond. How is he speaking to you in this moment through these teachings?

EXPLORE

Rauschenbusch, Walter. *Christianity and the Social Crisis in the 21st Century: The Classic that Woke Up the Church.* San Francisco: HarperOne, 2009.

24

As One Who Had Authority

WHILE IT MAY INITIALLY SEEM like an odd choice in a collection such as this, the following verses force us to ask: if Jesus is who we say he is, then do we truly ascribe to his words the weight they deserve?

> Now when Jesus saw the crowds, he went up on a mountainside and sat down. His disciples came to him, and he began to teach them.
> —MATTHEW 5:1–2 (NIV)

> When Jesus had finished saying these things, the crowds were amazed at his teaching, because he taught as one who had authority, and not as their teachers of the law. When Jesus came down from the mountainside, large crowds followed him.
> —MATTHEW 7:28–8:1 (NIV)

From escaping genocide at the hands of an evil king, in his flight to and return from Egypt, to his baptism in the Jordan River followed by forty days in the wilderness, the Exodus story echoes throughout the early life of Jesus. So, it is no accident when Jesus climbs a mountain, sits down, and begins to teach. For it was from a mountain that the newly freed Hebrew slaves found themselves in the presence of God, receiving from him the covenant and the law upon which their new society was to be based, as a light unto the nations. In this simple act, Jesus simultaneously embodies the role and authority of both God and Moses. Therefore, if Jesus is who we say he is, do we then ascribe to his words (the red letters) the true weight they deserve? Do we allow his teachings, particularly his Sermon on the

Mount, to function as "the constitution of the kingdom of God," as the law upon which we base our spiritual and social-political practices alike?[1]

Note: To speak of Jesus's words as the red letters is by no means to downplay the importance of Scripture in its totality, quite the contrary in fact. It is only through Scripture that we come to know Jesus and his role in fulfilling the mission of God. Rather, such a focus on the red letters recognizes Jesus for who he and the gospel writers explicitly say he is and takes seriously what Scripture actually expects of us as communities of faith. It is those who seek to dismiss, downplay, or reinterpret to the point of irrelevance the specific, concrete teachings of Jesus about which I am most worried.

REFLECT

- To what extent do the specific, concrete teachings of Jesus (the red letters) inform your discipleship practice and that of your faith community?
- How do you feel regarding the notion that Christianity has a "law," similar in certain respects to religions like Judaism or Islam?

PRAY

I am no longer my own, but yours. Put me to what you will; place me with whom you will. Put me to doing; put me to suffering. Let me be put to work for you or set aside for you, praised for you or criticized for you. Let me be full; let me be empty. Let me have all things; let me have nothing. I freely and fully surrender all things to your glory and service. And now, O wonderful and holy God, creator, redeemer, and sustainer, you are mine, and I am yours. So be it. And the covenant which I have made on earth, let it also be made in heaven. Amen.

—JOHN WESLEY (EIGHTEENTH CENTURY)

EXPLORE

McKnight, Scot. *Sermon on the Mount*. The Story of God Bible Commentary 21. Grand Rapids: Zondervan Academic, 2013.

Haddad, Elie, and Jesse Steven Wheeler. "Jesus Christ, King and Caliph: The Writings of Glen Stassen and Our Middle Eastern Communities." *Christian Ethics Today* 22:4 (2014) 16–20.

---

1. Stassen, *Living the Sermon*, Chap. 1.

25

Salty Torchbearers

UNDERSTANDABLY, THE CONFLUENCE OF FAITH and politics can be difficult to navigate. Some are adamant that such seemingly disparate paths must never cross. There can be no overlap. Others are essentially theocrats. The following passage, however, offers guidance in navigating such extremes, between the Scylla of sectarian withdrawal and Charybdis of theocratic authoritarianism:

> You are the salt of the earth. But if the salt loses its saltiness, how can it be made salty again? It is no longer good for anything, except to be thrown out and trampled underfoot.
>
> You are the light of the world. A town built on a hill cannot be hidden. Neither do people light a lamp and put it under a bowl. Instead they put it on its stand, and it gives light to everyone in the house.
>
> In the same way, let your light shine before others, that they may see your good deeds and glorify your Father in heaven.
>
> —MATTHEW 5:13–16 (NIV)

We see in Scripture that the powerful, distinctive, and at times overwhelming taste of salt serves as an image of covenant fidelity, of singular loyalty to the one true king. The people of God are to act different, look different, and be different. They are to live a life defined in all things by love of God and neighbor. We seek to model a new way of being not conformed to the destructive, violent, and sinful patterns of this world. Co-option by the powers that be (left, right, or center) results in the loss of our saltiness and a forfeiture of our distinctiveness as the people of God. Yet, to withdraw ourselves from the world in an ill-conceived and isolationist pursuit of purity is to miss the very point of our salvation.

As "the light of the world," it is imperative that we remain present and active in our communities, never fearing "the dark." Having been washed clean once and for all by the blood of Christ, we have zero fear of so-called "contamination." To be the light of the world is not to condemn, withdraw, or shy away from the world. But, it is to actively pursue the dark places, to willingly enter into places of pain and poverty, of illness and injustice, of violence and sin so that by our good deeds and sacrificial service—in imitation of the messiah himself—we might shine the light, love, justice, and peace of God's reign to those persons and places that need it most. As the watching world watches us, it is our hope that they cannot help but be drawn to the overwhelming light, justice, and love of our king and savior Jesus Christ.

REFLECT

- How have you understood the meaning of and relationship between "salt" and "light" in this passage? What are the possible consequences of leaning too much in the direction of "salt" on the one hand or of "light" on the other?

- What does it look like in practice for you and your faith community to live as both "salt" and "light" in your context? How can you hold simultaneously to your saltiness as a loyal citizen of God's kingdom and to your mission as torchbearer amid those situations of darkness and pain in urgent need of light?

PRAY

Disturb us, Lord, when we are too pleased with ourselves, when our dreams have come true because we dreamed too little, when we arrived safely because we sailed too close to the shore. Disturb us, Lord, when with the abundance of things we possess we have lost our thirst for the waters of life; having fallen in love with life, we have ceased to dream of eternity and in our efforts to build a new earth, we have allowed our vision of the new heaven to dim. Disturb us, Lord, to dare more boldly, to venture on wilder seas where storms will show your mastery; where losing sight of land, we shall find the stars. We ask you to push back the horizons of our hopes; and to push back the future in strength, courage, hope, and love. This we ask in the name of our captain, who is Jesus Christ.

Salty Torchbearers

—Attributed to Francis Drake (sixteenth century)

EXPLORE

Reimer, Johannes. *Missio Politica: The Mission of Church and Politics.* Carlisle: Langham Global Library, 2017.

Wheeler, Jesse Steven. "Alternate Light: Christian Witness in Imitation of Christ." *The IMES Blog.* Arab Baptist Theological Seminary (2014). IMES.blog.

26

Yes. No. Maybe?

It can seem at times as though ours is a socio-political culture drowning in hyperbole, misrepresentation, disinformation, half-truths, and outright lies. A healthier society, however, should be built upon trust, the basis of which is honesty. As informed by social psychology and political economics alike, this is as true for peacebuilding and political stability as is it for community development and economic growth.

> *"Blessed are the pure in heart, for they will see God."*
>
> —Matthew 5:8 (NRSV)

> *Again, you have heard that it was said to those of ancient times, "You shall not swear falsely, but carry out the vows you have made to the Lord." But I say to you, do not swear at all, either by heaven, for it is the throne of God, or by the earth, for it is his footstool, or by Jerusalem, for it is the city of the great King. And do not swear by your head, for you cannot make one hair white or black. Let your word be "Yes, Yes" or "No, No"; anything more than this comes from the evil one.*
>
> —Matthew 5:33–37 (NRSV)

The historical context for this passage involves a situation whereby the swearing of oaths was used often as a pretext for dishonesty and fraud (similar perhaps to our contractual "fine print"), as a means of manipulating others into trusting promises one has no intention of keeping. Naturally, such practices help cultivate a culture of mistrust. As Christian ethicists Glen Stassen and David Gushee tell us,

The very existence of an oath level of speech threatens to render (or unveil) everyday speech as less trustworthy . . .

The oath level really only exists because people cannot be counted on to speak truthfully under normal circumstances. Otherwise, there would be no need for it. But if people cannot be counted on to tell the truth when not under oath, then why should they be trusted to do so when they are under oath? If truthfulness, in and of itself, is not valued at all times, then no one's speech can be fully trusted, no matter how many Bibles the person swears on. And of course, the whole situation is worsened beyond repair if I then introduce various exceptions or escape clauses within the oath system that I do employ, or if I sometimes use oaths cynically to fool people into believing my lies.[1]

To escape this resulting pattern of misrepresentation and distrust, Jesus instructs us instead to speak truth in all circumstances. To devote ourselves to truth—letting our word be little more than a plainspoken "yes" or "no,"—is to render obsolete "oath-taking" and the dishonesty it represents. In this way, we hope to see the transformative truth of God's kingdom break through and clear away the web of lies that give shape to the political, economic, and socio-cultural discourses of our age.

REFLECT

- How have you understood the practice of swearing oaths? Are there areas in your life where you have been less than honest in your interactions or dealings with others?

- What is the relationship between truth-telling and trust in the establishment of a "healthy" society? How might a commitment to truth be seen as contributing to the manifestation of God's kingdom on earth as it is in heaven?

PRAY

Almighty God, you proclaim your truth in every age by many voices: Direct, in our time, we pray, those who speak where many listen and write what many read; that they may do their part in making the heart of this people wise, its mind sound, and its will righteous; to the honor of Jesus Christ our Lord. Amen.

—The Book of Common Prayer (1979)

---

1. Stassen and Gushee, *Kingdom Ethics*, 293.

EXPLORE

Walton, Jonathan P. *Twelve Lies that Hold America Captive: And the Truth that Sets Us Free*. Downers Grove: Intervarsity Press, 2019.

27

The Tyranny of Approval

Some religious leaders flock to power and influence like moths to a flame. You find them at Oval Office photo ops and national prayer break-fasts, on talk-radio shows and satellite television, or standing beside majority world dictators. For others, the primary temptation is approval or professional respect. These can be found in seminary halls and writing for erudite periodicals, or recording their latest podcast and virtue signaling on social media. Each, however, runs the serious risk of "institutional capture," of perpetuating or becoming tools of the powers and systems that they perhaps once sought to influence.

> *Blessed are the meek, for they will inherit the earth.*
> —Matthew 5:5 (NIV)

> *Be careful not to practice your righteousness in front of others to be seen by them. If you do, you will have no reward from your Father in heaven. So when you give to the needy, do not announce it with trumpets, as the hypocrites do in the synagogues and on the streets, to be honored by others. Truly I tell you, they have received their reward in full. But when you give to the needy, do not let your left hand know what your right hand is doing, so that your giving may be in secret.*
>
> *And when you pray, do not be like the hypocrites, for they love to pray standing in the synagogues and on the street corners to be seen by others. Truly I tell you, they have received their reward in full. But when you pray, go into your room, close the door and pray to your Father, who is unseen. Then your Father, who sees what is done in secret, will reward you. And when you pray, do not keep on*

> *babbling like pagans, for they think they will be heard because of their many words. Do not be like them, for your Father knows what you need before you ask him.*
>
> —Matthew 6:1–8 (NIV)

> *When you fast, do not look somber as the hypocrites do, for they disfigure their faces to show others they are fasting. Truly I tell you, they have received their reward in full. But when you fast, put oil on your head and wash your face, so that it will not be obvious to others that you are fasting, but only to your Father, who is unseen; and your Father, who sees what is done in secret, will reward you.*
>
> —Matthew 5:16–18 (NIV)

Many of us live and die for the approval or respect of others. As we obsess over how we look through the eyes of others, we forget to see ourselves through the eyes of God. And in response, our public lives begin to resemble a performance. In seeking status or saving face, thousands of decisions are made each day in the service of crafting a public persona, from the clothes we wear and the cars we drive to the careers we pursue and the causes we champion. Politics is all about performance. Even our spiritual life becomes a performance. Consequently, a schism develops between our inner, private selves and our publicly cultivated personas. While some seek adoration and the social power that comes with it, others live with the pain of failing to live up to the illusory projections of others.

Meanwhile, there are those who would manipulate our insecurities for their own personal, social, financial, or political gain. This is done through the promotion of conspicuous consumption, cultish notions of identity, purpose, and belonging, xenophobic militarism, dehumanizing institutional and corporate cultures, ideological loyalty tests, or even promises of spiritual power and divine blessing. However, finding rest within God's approving gaze and the blessed assurance of Christ's unending love and unmerited grace provides for us the psychosocial security required to live as whole, integral persons. And, as persons of integrity, we can resist the tyranny of approval and the corrupting influences of those powers and systems that would seek to capture us for their own destructive ends.

REFLECT

- How and to what extent, if any, have you found yourself captive to the "tyranny of approval?"

- How might our respective societies look if we made decisions as individuals and communities secure in the love and acceptance of God, as opposed to the watchful eyes of others?

PRAY

> *Govern everything by your wisdom, O Lord, so that my soul may always be serving you in the way you will and not as I choose. Let me die to myself so that I may serve you; let me live to you who are life itself. Amen.*
> —Theresa of Avila (sixteenth century)

EXPLORE

Volf, Miroslav. *Free of Charge: Giving and Forgiving in a Culture Stripped of Grace.* Grand Rapids: Zondervan, 2006.

28

Keeping Up with the Kingdom

THE FOLLOWING PASSAGES HIGHLIGHT THE socio-economic imperatives of God's just reign:

> God blesses those who hunger and thirst for justice, for they will be satisfied.
>
> —MATTHEW 5:6 (NLT)

> Don't store up treasures here on earth, where moths eat them and rust destroys them, and where thieves break in and steal. Store your treasures in heaven, where moths and rust cannot destroy, and thieves do not break in and steal. Wherever your treasure is, there the desires of your heart will also be.
>
> Your eye is like a lamp that provides light for your body. When your eye is healthy, your whole body is filled with light. But when your eye is unhealthy, your whole body is filled with darkness. And if the light you think you have is actually darkness, how deep that darkness is!
>
> No one can serve two masters. For you will hate one and love the other; you will be devoted to one and despise the other. You cannot serve God and be enslaved to money.
>
> —MATTHEW 6:19–24 (NLT)

So much of our socio-economic life consists in an unsustainable cycle of acquisition, consumption, and waste. Moreover, the continual acquisition of ever more stuff results in the establishment of ever greater security measures needed to partition off and protect "our treasure" from the increasing covetousness of those around us. So, we build walls. But, walling off our stuff has the unfortunate effect of walling us away from our neighbors, resulting in an ever-widening estrangement between ourselves and our socio-economic others.

The abuse of zoning laws, homeowners associations, and gated communities; private security firms, racialized policing, and territorial militias; national borders, citizenship laws, and militarism; or even fashion, etiquette, and social status, are each but strands in a web of exclusion we collectively spin. In the biting fourth century words of Ambrose of Milan:

> The large rooms of which you are so proud are in fact your shame. They are big enough to hold crowds—and also big enough to shut out the voice of the poor! . . . You clothe your walls and you strip human beings. The poor man cries before your house, and you pay no attention. There is your brother, naked, crying, and you worry about an attractive floor covering![1] . . . The people are starving, and you close up your granaries. The people are wailing, and you twist your jeweled ring. Unhappy man, in whose power it lies to save the lives of so many from death, and there is no will to do so!"[2]

To begin clearing away the web, we must clean our eyes of both covetousness on the one hand and suspicion on the other. For to store up treasures in heaven is to trust in the red letters of Jesus as opposed to the red lines, to find freedom and satisfaction in a life of generosity and singular devotion to the advancement of God's just reign on earth as it is in heaven.

REFLECT

- How intentional have you been in monitoring your consumption and purchasing practices?
- How might "storing up treasures in heaven" instead of on earth help us to break free of the cycles of increasing alienation and estrangement that defines so much of our socio-economic life?

PRAY

> *Grant, O God, that your holy and life giving Spirit may so move every human heart [and especially the hearts of the people of this land], that barriers which divide us may crumble, suspicions disappear,*

---

1. Ambrose, *De Nabuthe Jezraelite*, §13.56, quoted in Adams, *CQOD*, lines 2–6.
2. Ambrose, "On Naboth," §13.56.

and hatreds cease; that our divisions being healed, we may live in justice and peace; through Jesus Christ our Lord. Amen.

—The Book of Common Prayer (1979)

EXPLORE

Myers, Bryant L. *Engaging Globalization: The Poor, Christian Mission, and Our Hyperconnected World.* Grand Rapids: Baker Academic, 2017.

———. *Walking with the Poor: Principles and Practices of Transformational Development.* Revised and Expanded Edition. Maryknoll: Orbis, 2011.

29

Look. Notice. Desire.

EXPLORING THE SOCIO-ECONOMIC IMPLICATIONS OF God's kingdom, we continue today in the Sermon on the Mount:

> No one can serve two masters. Either you will hate the one and love the other, or you will be loyal to the one and have contempt for the other. You cannot serve God and wealth. Therefore, I say to you, don't worry about your life, what you'll eat or what you'll drink, or about your body, what you'll wear. Isn't life more than food and the body more than clothes?
>
> Look at the birds in the sky. They don't sow seed or harvest grain or gather crops into barns. Yet your heavenly Father feeds them. Aren't you worth much more than they are? Who among you by worrying can add a single moment to your life? And why do you worry about clothes?
>
> Notice how the lilies in the field grow. They don't wear themselves out with work, and they don't spin cloth. But I say to you that even Solomon in all of his splendor wasn't dressed like one of these. If God dresses grass in the field so beautifully, even though it's alive today and tomorrow it's thrown into the furnace, won't God do much more for you, you people of weak faith?
>
> Therefore, don't worry and say, "What are we going to eat?" or "What are we going to drink?" or "What are we going to wear?" Gentiles long for all these things. Your heavenly Father knows that you need them.
>
> Instead, desire first and foremost God's kingdom and God's righteousness, and all these things will be given to you as well. Therefore, stop worrying about tomorrow, because tomorrow will worry about itself. Each day has enough trouble of its own.

Serving a Crucified King

—Matthew 6:24–34 (CEB)

It must be emphasized that this passage doesn't consist of an impossible prohibition on anxiety, an emotional state as natural to some of us as breathing. None should ever be made to feel guilty or experience shame over something so often beyond one's control. Instead, we are invited to take comfort in the promises of God's providential care. What this teaching does consist of, however, is a warning against the impossible situation of attempting to serve both God and wealth. Within creation, God has provided us with adequate resources to meet everyone's needs should we collectively and proactively make it so.

But, in our anxiety, we hoard. We reserve for ourselves that which could have been better used by another who must now go without. By doing so, we so often forget that all wealth belongs not to us, but God, and we seem to lose our ability to give generously. Immoral actions at the personal and interpersonal levels converge, feeding into the establishment of unjust macro-level systems (which in turn give shape to our micro-level decision making). And this ultimately results in a misallocation of resources and the exploitation of our global neighbors—as evidenced especially by both the contemporary agriculture and fashion industries. Instead, trust God. Live simply. Pursue the justice and righteousness of his kingdom on earth as it is in heaven. And you will find satisfaction.

REFLECT

- Are there ways in which you find yourself attempting to serve both God and wealth? Are there other possible idols in your life competing for your allegiance and dividing your attention?

- To what extent do prevalent socio-economic or political ideologies force us to divide our loyalties between God and wealth, or anything and anyone else demanding our loyalty apart from God? How might the teachings of Jesus free us from the anxiety of dual allegiances?

PRAY

Find comfort in the following benediction of Francis de Sales:

> *Do not look forward in fear to the changes in life; rather, look to them with full hope that as they arise, God, whose very own you are, will lead you safely through all things; and when you cannot stand it, God will carry you in his arms. Do not fear what may happen*

tomorrow; the same understanding Father who cares for you today will take care of you then and every day. He will either shield you from suffering or will give you unfailing strength to bear it. Be at peace, and put aside all anxious thoughts and imaginations.

—Francis de Sales (eighteenth century)

EXPLORE

Shaw, Karen L. H. *Wealth and Piety: Middle Eastern Perspectives for Expat Workers.* Pasadena: William Carey, 2018.

30

Drink the Cup

It is my conviction that faith is inherently political, relating as it does to issues of ultimate loyalty and the ethical ordering of our communal life. Central to this is the question of power, its proper usage and distribution. The following story is illustrative:

> As Jesus was going up to Jerusalem, he took the twelve disciples aside privately and told them what was going to happen to him. "Listen," he said, "we're going up to Jerusalem, where the Son of Man will be betrayed to the leading priests and the teachers of religious law. They will sentence him to die. Then they will hand him over to the Romans to be mocked, flogged with a whip, and crucified. But on the third day he will be raised from the dead."
>
> Then the mother of James and John, the sons of Zebedee, came to Jesus with her sons. She knelt respectfully to ask a favor. "What is your request?" he asked.
>
> She replied, "In your kingdom, please let my two sons sit in places of honor next to you, one on your right and the other on your left."
>
> But Jesus answered by saying to them, "You don't know what you are asking! Are you able to drink from the bitter cup of suffering I am about to drink?"
>
> "Oh yes," they replied, "we are able!"
>
> Jesus told them, "You will indeed drink from my bitter cup. But I have no right to say who will sit on my right or my left. My Father has prepared those places for the ones he has chosen."
>
> When the ten other disciples heard what James and John had asked, they were indignant. But Jesus called them together and said, "You know that the rulers in this world lord it over their people, and officials flaunt their authority over those under them. But among

you it will be different. Whoever wants to be a leader among you must be your servant, and whoever wants to be first among you must become your slave. For even the Son of Man came not to be served but to serve others and to give his life as a ransom for many."

—MATTHEW 20:17–28 (NLT)

As paraphrased by N. T. Wright, "The kings of the earth exercise power one way, by lording it over their subjects, but Jesus's followers are going to do it the other way, the way of the servant."[1] Too often, however, we align ourselves with the dictators or ruling powers of the day for the sake of political expediency and personal security. We support racial profiling and draconian policing at home and militarism abroad in the name of national security. We support a socio-economic system that ensures the racial, ethnic, or sectarian dominance of one particular group at the expense of another. And in doing so, we become guilty ourselves of exploiting our social power at the expense of our sisters and brothers. We carry their blood on our hands.

That the religious leaders of his day, after declaring they had "no king but Caesar,"[2] handed Jesus over for execution as a traitor and political insurgent is but an illustration of what happens when we don't consider the moral magnitude of such alliances. This, however, is not the way of Christ. For with the death and resurrection of Christ Jesus, an instrument of imperial domination becomes in biblical imagination the ultimate symbol of divine love and the power-reversing means by which God reigns. To serve the crucified king is to surrender our claim to earthly domination as we trust in his ultimate lordship. In doing so, we offer the world a new way forward, the narrow path of self-sacrificial, all-embracing love.

REFLECT

- Imagine yourself in the position of James and John. Would you be willing and able to "drink from the same cup" as Christ? What lessons can be learned for today from the fact that Christ's death came at the hands of the religious as well as the imperial authorities of his day?

- What does Jesus's statement that "the rulers in this world lord it over their people, and officials flaunt their authority over those under them. But among you it will be different" teach us about the proper

---

1. Wright, *God Became King,* 139.
2. John 19:15 (NIV)

use of power? What is the relationship between power and the gospel message?

PRAY

Lord Jesus, we deceive ourselves too often into thinking we know what it means to drink your cup. And yet, we idolize security and comfort. We yearn for status and crave having authority. Teach us to follow in your path, to serve you in our service to others, and divest ourselves from the power, however great or little, to which we so jealously cling. May we place our trust in you alone and walk behind you on the narrow path of self-sacrificial, all-embracing love. In your holy name we pray, Lord Jesus. Amen.

—A Prayer for Faith (original)

EXPLORE

Weaver, Dorothy Jean. *The Irony of Power: The Politics of God within Matthew's Narrative*. Eugene: Pickwick, 2017.

Wheeler, Jesse Steven. "Christ-Centered Witness and the Proper Use of Power." *The IMES Blog*. Arab Baptist Theological Seminary (2013). IMES.blog.

31

As I Have Done

A CENTRAL MOTIF RUNNING THROUGHOUT the pages of Scripture is that of power. In the gospels, we find that Jesus consistently upends our presuppositions regarding its proper usage. This is because questions of power are central to understanding the gospel of the crucified king.

> *Before the Passover celebration, Jesus knew that his hour had come to leave this world and return to his Father. He had loved his disciples during his ministry on earth, and now he loved them to the very end. It was time for supper, and the devil had already prompted Judas, son of Simon Iscariot, to betray Jesus. Jesus knew that the Father had given him authority over everything and that he had come from God and would return to God. So he got up from the table, took off his robe, wrapped a towel around his waist, and poured water into a basin. Then he began to wash the disciples' feet, drying them with the towel he had around him.*
>
> *When Jesus came to Simon Peter, Peter said to him, "Lord, are you going to wash my feet?"*
>
> *Jesus replied, "You don't understand now what I am doing, but someday you will."*
>
> *"No," Peter protested, "you will never ever wash my feet!"*
>
> *Jesus replied, "Unless I wash you, you won't belong to me."*
>
> *Simon Peter exclaimed, "Then wash my hands and head as well, Lord, not just my feet!" . . .*
>
> *After washing their feet, he put on his robe again and sat down and asked, "Do you understand what I was doing? You call me 'Teacher' and 'Lord,' and you are right, because that's what I am. And since I, your Lord and Teacher, have washed your feet, you ought to wash each other's feet. I have given you an example to follow. Do as*

> *I have done to you. I tell you the truth, slaves are not greater than their master. Nor is the messenger more important than the one who sends the message. Now that you know these things, God will bless you for doing them.*
>
> —John 13:3–10; 13–17 (NLT)

Key to understanding the actions of Jesus is the knowledge that in him has been invested authority and power over all things. He is quite literally the sovereign of all creation. And, it is on this basis that the king of the cosmos takes upon himself the role not merely of servant but that of humiliated foot washer, an act virtually inconceivable within the honor and shame bound context of first-century Palestine. Even today, anything associated in West Asian culture with the foot carries with it a sense of impurity, insult, and shame. From personal experience, I was deeply moved each year by how the faculty at the Arab Baptist Theological Seminary in Lebanon would conduct a ceremony to clean and shine the shoes of its graduating students (a role reversal of profound impact) and present to each a towel reminding them to follow the counter-cultural example set by Jesus. In a world rife with the abuse of power and the status that comes with it, the kingdom of God rests upon the self-sacrificial love and humiliating example of Christ, who would soon after hang naked upon the cross for all to see. In this act is found the true power of the gospel.

REFLECT

- Imagine yourself as a disciple in the room with Jesus on the eve of his crucifixion. How would you feel about and react to his surprising actions that night, alongside his subsequent request for you to go and do likewise? Would you have the courage to humiliate yourself in such a manner for the sake of the kingdom?
- What lessons might be learned for today concerning the true cost of Christian discipleship, especially as it collides with human ambition and pride?

PRAY

> *Jesus, my feet are dirty. Come even as a slave to me; pour water into your bowl; come and wash my feet. In asking such a thing I know I am overbold, but I dread what was threatened when you said to me,*

As I Have Done

"If I do not wash your feet I have no fellowship with you." Wash my feet then, because I long for your companionship.
— Origen (third century)

EXPLORE

Andrews, Jonathan, ed. *The Missiology behind the Story: Voices from the Arab World.* The Institute of Middle East Studies Series. Carlisle: Langham Global Library, 2019.

32

The Same Attitude

WHILE THE FOLLOWING PASSAGE SPEAKS to the issue of power's proper usage, it also speaks profoundly to our relations with one another, offering a reorientation to life for those who would follow Christ. Furthermore, it presents an amazing message for approaching contemporary socio-cultural realities:

> *Above all, you must live as citizens of heaven, conducting yourselves in a manner worthy of the good news about Christ. Then, whether I come and see you again or only hear about you, I will know that you are standing together with one spirit and one purpose, fighting together for the faith, which is the good news . . .*
>
> *For you have been given not only the privilege of trusting in Christ but also the privilege of suffering for him. We are in this struggle together. You have seen my struggle in the past, and you know that I am still in the midst of it.*
>
> *Is there any encouragement from belonging to Christ? Any comfort from his love? Any fellowship together in the Spirit? Are your hearts tender and compassionate? Then make me truly happy by agreeing wholeheartedly with each other, loving one another, and working together with one mind and purpose.*
>
> *Don't be selfish; don't try to impress others. Be humble, thinking of others as better than yourselves. Don't look out only for your own interests, but take an interest in others, too.*
>
> *You must have the same attitude that Christ Jesus had.*
>
> *Though he was God, he did not think of equality with God as something to cling to. Instead, he gave up his divine privileges; he took the humble position of a slave and was born as a human being.*

The Same Attitude

When he appeared in human form, he humbled himself in obedience to God and died a criminal's death on a cross.

Therefore, God elevated him to the place of highest honor and gave him the name above all other names, that at the name of Jesus every knee should bow, in heaven and on earth and under the earth, and every tongue declare that Jesus Christ is Lord, to the glory of God the Father.

—Philippians 1:27; 1:29—2:9 (NLT)

REFLECT

Sit with this passage for a few minutes in silence. Reflect on the magnitude of the apostles' words, upon heavenly citizenship, suffering, and what it means for Jesus to have emptied himself of his divine privileges. Likewise, ask yourself what it looks like in practice for you to "have the same attitude as Christ Jesus," in the home or at the office, in business or politics, or within the church and your spiritual life?

PRAY

Now, slowly read through the passage again. Focus on the word or phrase that most convicts you or the concept you find most troubling. Pray over it. Ask the Lord to guide and direct you with regard to how he might be speaking through it to you in this moment. Consider how the lessons of this passage regarding the proper use and exercise of power might be lived out practically in all areas of your life.

EXPLORE

Gushee, David P., and Reggie L. Williams, eds. *Justice and the Way of Jesus: Christian Ethics and the Incarnational Discipleship of Glen Stassen*. Maryknoll: Orbis, 2020.

33

Prayer as Political

PRAYER, THOUGH WE MAY NOT always recognize it as such, is a deeply political act. Today, we need prayer as much as ever, trusting in God's justice and deliverance as we live through circumstances beyond our control. In the words of Jesus:

> *This, then, is how you should pray: "Our Father in heaven, hallowed be your name. Your kingdom come, your will be done, on earth as it is in heaven. Give us today our daily bread. And forgive us our debts, as we also have forgiven our debtors. And lead us not into testing, but deliver us from the evil one."*
>
> *For if you forgive other people when they sin against you, your heavenly Father will also forgive you. But if you do not forgive others their sins, your Father will not forgive your sins.*
>
> —MATTHEW 6:9–15 (NIV)

The Lord's Prayer is at its core about the kingship of God, a recognition that there can truly be no kingdom without a king. Our prayer acts as a declaration of allegiance to God's holy name as we pray that his reign of joy, justice, and peace (his will) be established on earth as it is already in heaven. Central to this kingdom vision is that our essential needs are met, that our debts to God and others are forgiven, and that we would find deliverance from the evil to which we find ourselves captive—that earth begins to resemble heaven. As we pledge our allegiance to God's holy name, we actualize the kingdom in our midst. That through it all we are invited to call the king of all creation "our father" is uniquely spectacular. In our prayer we recognize that while the kings and queens of this earth may currently rule at God's pleasure, they certainly don't rule on his behalf. And, they will be held fully accountable one day for their disobedience, injustice, idolatry, and violence. For to God alone belong the kingdom, the power, and the glory.

REFLECT

- How might our prayer life change if we were to understand it as a political act, as a declaration of allegiance?
- Which of your socio-political loyalties or economic practices is called into question by this prayer? Be specific and consider policies or practices upheld by your political party or affiliation.

PRAY

Spend some time slowly praying through each line of the Lord's Prayer, seeing it as a declaration of loyalty, a pledge of allegiance, to the just reign of God:

> *Our Father in heaven,*
> *hallowed be your name.*
> *Your kingdom come,*
> *your will be done,*
> *on earth as it is in heaven.*
> *Give us today our daily bread.*
> *And forgive us our debts,*
> *as we also have forgiven our debtors.*
> *And lead us not into testing,*
> *but deliver us from the evil one.*
> *Amen.*
>
> —Matthew 6:9–13 (NIV)

EXPLORE

Wright, N. T. *The Lord and His Prayer*. Grand Rapids: Eerdmans, 2014.

34

Misplaced Allegiances

PERHAPS FEW OTHER PASSAGES SPEAK to the political nature of prayer as strongly as the following. It forces us to ask, "To whom are we loyal?" And, it reminds us that in times of need or fear, when we are tempted to put our hope in less-than-trustworthy sources, we can place our trust in the king:

> *Don't give to dogs what belongs to God. They will only turn and attack you. Don't throw pearls down in front of pigs. They will trample all over them.*
>
> *Ask, and you will receive. Search, and you will find. Knock, and the door will be opened for you. Everyone who asks will receive. Everyone who searches will find. And the door will be opened for everyone who knocks. Would any of you give your hungry child a stone, if the child asked for some bread? Would you give your child a snake if the child asked for a fish? As bad as you are, you still know how to give good gifts to your children. But your heavenly Father is even more ready to give good things to people who ask.*
>
> —MATTHEW 7:6–11 (CEV)

> *For without consulting me, you have gone down to Egypt for help. You have put your trust in Pharaoh's protection. You have tried to hide in his shade. But by trusting Pharaoh, you will be humiliated, and by depending on him, you will be disgraced. For though his power extends to Zoan and his officials have arrived in Hanes, all who trust in him will be ashamed. He will not help you. Instead, he will disgrace you.*
>
> —ISAIAH 30:2–5 (NLT)

Misplaced Allegiances

> *The Lord God is waiting to show how kind he is and to have pity on you. The Lord always does right; he blesses those who trust him. People of Jerusalem, you don't need to cry anymore. The Lord is kind, and as soon as he hears your cries for help, he will come.*
>
> —Isaiah 30:18–19 (CEV)

Taken in isolation, many have wondered as to the meaning behind Jesus's instruction not to "throw your pearls before swine." Some have even read xenophobic or sectarian intentions into the passage, since Jesus's contemporaries would have immediately recognized "dogs" and "pigs" as referring to gentiles.[1] However, digging deeper into the textual and socio-historical context allows us to recognize this as being instead a warning against misplaced loyalty, a misguided trust in the seductive power of Roman imperial might or Hellenistic culture (and their modern equivalents!).[2] Just as each of us would take extraordinary care in choosing a daycare provider for our children, never "giving to them a snake when they ask for a fish," so too must we take great care concerning those to whom we entrust our very lives and in what we place our ultimate allegiance.

While Jesus often warned against the "zealot option" of the violent revolutionary—soon to result in Jerusalem's destruction at the hands of Rome—this passage serves as a rebuke against the temple establishment.[3] It is an admonishment against those collaborators with "no king but Caesar"[4] who put their trust in an imperial power that would soon turn on them, trampling them under feet the moment it was in their interest or convenience to do so. The Egyptian empire, as alluded to above, was infamous for betraying its allies in their time of need. Rome, for its part, would lay waste to the temple compound so completely that "not one stone will be left on top of another."[5] For this reason, entrust your allegiance to the heavenly father who is worthy of your trust.

REFLECT

- Who, or what, competes for your loyalty and allegiance? Which among these might be understood as being particularly destructive?

---

1. Hagner, *Matthew 1–13*, 171; McKnight, *Sermon*, 237.
2. Stassen and Gushee, *Kingdom Ethics*, 347.
3. Stassen and Gushee, *Kingdom Ethics*, 349.
4. John 19:15 (NIV)
5. See Luke 21:6 (NLT)

- What do you think of as being contemporary equivalents to "the seductive power of Roman imperial might or Hellenistic culture?"

PRAY

God, great governor of the world, we pray to you for all who hold public office and power, for the life, the welfare, and the virtue of the people are in their hands to make or to mar. We remember with shame that in the past the mighty have prayed on the labors of the poor; that they have laid nations in the dust by their oppression, and have thwarted the love and the prayers of your servants. We bless you that the new spirit of democracy has touched even the kings of the earth. We rejoice that by the free institutions of our country the tyrannous instincts of the strong may be curbed and turned to the patient service of the commonwealth. Strengthen the sense of duty in our political life.

Grant that the servants of the state may feel ever more deeply that any diversion of their public powers for private ends is a betrayal of their country. Purge our cities and states and nation of the deep causes of corruption which have so often made sin profitable and uprightness hard. Bring to an end the stale days of party cunning. Breathe a new spirit into all our nation. Lift us from the dust and mire of the past that we may gird ourselves for a new day's work. Give our leaders a new vision of the possible future of our country and set their hearts on fire with large resolves. Raise up a new generation of public women and men, who will have the faith and daring of the kingdom of God in their hearts, and who will enlist for life in a holy warfare for the freedom and rights of the people.

—Walter Rauschenbusch (1910)

EXPLORE

Stassen, Glen H. *A Thicker Jesus: Incarnational Discipleship in a Secular Age.* Louisville: Westminster John Knox, 2012.

35

Tested Loyalties

THE STORY OF DANIEL EPITOMIZES the prophet Jeremiah's injunction to faithfully "seek the peace of the city to which you are sent." That being said, the following passage illustrates perfectly the power of "prayer, as a political act" when our ultimate loyalties are tested:

> Darius the Mede decided to divide the kingdom into 120 provinces, and he appointed a high officer to rule over each province. The king also chose Daniel and two others as administrators to supervise the high officers and protect the king's interests. Daniel soon proved himself more capable than all the other administrators and high officers. Because of Daniel's great ability, the king made plans to place him over the entire empire.
>
> Then the other administrators and high officers began searching for some fault in the way Daniel was handling government affairs, but they couldn't find anything to criticize or condemn. He was faithful, always responsible, and completely trustworthy. So they concluded, "Our only chance of finding grounds for accusing Daniel will be in connection with the rules of his religion."
>
> So the administrators and high officers went to the king and said, "Long live King Darius! We are all in agreement—we administrators, officials, high officers, advisers, and governors—that the king should make a law that will be strictly enforced. Give orders that for the next thirty days any person who prays to anyone, divine or human—except to you, Your Majesty—will be thrown into the den of lions. And now, Your Majesty, issue and sign this law so it cannot be changed, an official law of the Medes and Persians that cannot be revoked." So King Darius signed the law.

> But when Daniel learned that the law had been signed, he went home and knelt down as usual in his upstairs room, with its windows open toward Jerusalem. He prayed three times a day, just as he had always done, giving thanks to his God. Then the officials went together to Daniel's house and found him praying and asking for God's help. So they went straight to the king and reminded him about his law. "Did you not sign a law that for the next thirty days any person who prays to anyone, divine or human—except to you, Your Majesty—will be thrown into the den of lions?"
>
> —Daniel 6:1–12 (NLT)

In the actions of the prophet Daniel we find perfectly illustrated the imperative to live as "salt and light," to be "in, but not of" the world as the often-misunderstood expression goes. In his allegiance to God, Daniel served the people of the realm to the best of his ability and with the utmost integrity. However, when the regime overstepped its bounds by asking far more than that to which it was entitled, Daniel unabashedly continued to pledge allegiance in prayer to his one true king. And, he willingly laid down his life in faithfulness. What we observe in this passage is the blatant manipulation of religious devotion for the pursuit and maintenance of power, alongside a human king under the destructive delusion that his power made him somehow worthy of the people's worship and praise. In their hubris, the powers that be—kings, presidents, nation-states, corporate boards, institutional bureaucrats, and religious leaders alike—demand our allegiance, our lives, and even at times our worship. This deadly combination is referred to as "imperial religion." It is the essence of idolatry. And, it's what ultimately led to the cross.

REFLECT

- What would it mean for you today to reject the idols of imperial religion and bow only before God? What steps can you take to imitate Daniel's courage?
- In what ways does Daniel epitomize "salt and light" within his Babylonian context? What lessons might be drawn from his example for today?

PRAY

To you, Lord, do I lift up my soul. My God, I trust in you; let me not be ashamed. Lord, you that bearest rule, Lord of heaven and earth, I call you Lord, though I am not worthy to be called your servant; for from my youth I did not serve you, but your enemy, the devil; him I served diligently; nevertheless, I do not doubt your grace; for I find in the word of your truth that you are a bountiful, rich Lord to all those who call upon you. Therefore, I call unto you; Lord hear me; hear me, Lord! With full confidence and assurance, I lift up, not my head or my hands as the hypocrites do . . . but my soul.

I lifted up my heart . . . alone to you, for you are our Lord and Father. You are our redeemer; this is your name, from days past. Hence it is, dear Lord, that I trust in you, for I truly know that you are a faithful God over all who trust in you. If I am in darkness, you are my light; if am I in prison, you are with me; if I am forsaken, you are my comfort; if I am in death, you are my life; if they curse me, you bless; if they grieve me, you comfort; if they will slay me, you will raise me up; and if I walk in the dark valley, you will ever be with me. It is right, Lord, that I lift up my grieved and miserable soul to you, trust in your promise, and am not ashamed.

—Menno Simons (sixteenth century)

EXPLORE

Ramachandra, Vinoth. *Gods that Fail: Modern Idolatry and Christian Mission.* Revised Edition. Eugene: Wipf & Stock, 2016.

Andrews, Jonathan, ed. *The Church in Disorienting Times: Leading Prophetically through Adversity.* Institute of Middle East Studies Series. Carlisle: Langham Global Library, 2018.

36

Blind to Our Blindness

IT'S EASY TO FIND FAULT in others, but it can be incredibly difficult to admit fault in ourselves. This unfortunate reality lies at the heart of sectarianism, racism and bigotry, hyper-partisanship, nationalism, and most other forms of social othering. In fact, so much conflict in our world results from a severe shortage of critical self-examination.

> *Do not judge others, and you will not be judged. For you will be treated as you treat others. The standard you use in judging is the standard by which you will be judged. And why worry about a speck in your friend's eye when you have a log in your own? How can you think of saying to your friend, "Let me help you get rid of that speck in your eye," when you can't see past the log in your own eye? Hypocrite! First get rid of the log in your own eye; then you will see well enough to deal with the speck in your friend's eye.*
>
> —MATTHEW 7:1–5 (NLT)

Contrary to popular assumption, this passage is not an exhortation to forgo discernment with regard to the actions and intentions of others. In fact, we are instructed elsewhere to be "as shrewd as serpents and as harmless as doves."[1] But, to paraphrase Jesus, "if we dish it out, then we better be prepared to take it." The problem is that we so easily and so often find fault in others yet fail to recognize our own myriad faults as they relate to race, religion, socio-economic or migration status, and the like. To this end, we construct self-serving narratives and ideological, even theological, justifications to espouse our own imagined innocence.

1. Matthew 10:16 (NLT)

At the same time, we promote the "fully-justifiable" mistreatment of others, leading to the rationalization of violence in a multitude of contexts. We fail to realize that the logs protruding from our eyes are even a problem! As such, we must engage in critical self-examination as individuals and socio-cultural communities. In this way, we can begin to recognize and remove the logs from our eyes. Then, and only then, can we credibly speak to the faults we find in others. What we so often come to learn, however, after engaging in the hard work of exposing and re-examining our own faults, prejudices, and historic injustices, is that we simply no longer worry that much anymore about the "specks" we may find in the eyes of another.

REFLECT

- Do you ever find yourself focusing on the faults of others without first examining your own?
- Which self-serving historical narratives and ideological or theological justifications do you find commonplace within your own community, society, or nation? What steps might be taken to catalyze a transformation in thinking and practice?

PRAY

Gracious Father, we pray for your church. Fill it with all truth, in all truth, with all peace. Where it is corrupt, purify it; where it is in error, direct it; where in anything it is amiss, reform it. Where it is right, strengthen it; where it is in want, provide for it; where it is divided, reunite it; for the sake of Jesus Christ your son, our savior. Amen.

—THE BOOK OF COMMON PRAYER (1979)

EXPLORE

Fiske, Alan Page, and Tage Shakti Rai. *Virtuous Violence: Hurting and Killing to Create, Sustain, End, and Honor Social Relationships.* Cambridge: Cambridge University Press, 2014.

Smith, Kay Higuera, Jayachitra Lalitha, and L. Daniel Hawk, eds. *Evangelical Postcolonial Conversations: Global Awakenings in Theology and Praxis.* Downers Grove: IVP Academic, 2014.

37

A Holy Kiss

IN SITUATIONS OF CONFLICT, THE journey towards authentic reconciliation requires that the often disparate demands of truth, mercy, justice, and peace each be satisfied:

> *Surely his salvation is near to them that fear him: that glory may dwell in our land. Mercy and truth have met each other; justice and peace have kissed.*
>
> —PSALM 85:9–10 (DRB)

> *So then, if anyone is in Christ, that person is part of the new creation. The old things have gone away, and look, new things have arrived!*
> *All of these new things are from God, who reconciled us to himself through Christ and who gave us the ministry of reconciliation. In other words, God was reconciling the world to himself through Christ, by not counting people's sins against them. He has trusted us with this message of reconciliation.*
> *So we are ambassadors who represent Christ. God is negotiating with you through us. We beg you as Christ's representatives, "Be reconciled to God!"*
>
> —2 CORINTHIANS 5:17–20 (CEB)

Lebanese scholar-peacebuilder Martin Accad speaks of the *kerygma* ("proclamation" in Greek) as "God's gracious and positive invitation of humanity into relationship with himself through Jesus."[1] This loving invitation to restored relationship provides the foundation for all Christ-centered

---

1. Accad, "Christian Attitudes," Chap. 1.

reconciliation efforts. For our restored relationship with God can never be divorced from the outward pursuit of reconciliation, be it interpersonal, interethnic, international, or even interfaith. So, we commit ourselves to the difficult task of reconciliation: the comprehensive restoration of those shattered relationships that so define our fallen world.[2]

However, experience tells us that the pursuit of peace without regard for justice is merely another name for pacification, the perpetuation of an ultimately oppressive status quo. Meanwhile, to pursue justice without a mind for peace repeatedly provides the rationale for engaging in or perpetrating violent action. Likewise, mercy without truth demands nothing in the way of repentance and becomes little more than an invitation for ongoing abuse. Finally, to seek after truth without a heart for mercy breeds anger and can have the effect of drowning out alternative perspectives. As respected Mennonite peacebuilder John Paul Lederach tells us,

> Reconciliation requires us to take up the primary practical task of creating the dynamic social space where Truth, Mercy, Justice, and Peace can genuinely meet and wrestle things out . . .
>
> Too often in the midst of conflict, we take these social energies . . . as contradictory forces . . . They are seen as pitted against each other. Those who cry out for Truth and Justice are taken as adversaries of those who plead for Mercy and Peace, and they often understand themselves that same way.
>
> The vision of thewpsalmist is different. Reconciliation is possible only as each sees the place and need for the other."[3]

"As we deal with conflict this way," Lederach concludes, "God reveals the road to reconciliation."[4] Central, therefore, to our political mission as kingdom citizens is the establishment of such sacred spaces where the demands of justice, peace, mercy, and truth can be adequately and authentically addressed. For it is the very face of God that we find in the face of our enemy.[5]

REFLECT

- Do you find yourself identifying with or naturally gravitating to one or another of the "social energies" of Mercy, Truth, Justice, and Peace? For what reasons do you think this is so?

2. Kärkkäinen, *Reconciliation*, 364.
3. Lederach, *Reconcile*, 91.
4. Lederach, *Reconcile*, 92.
5. Genesis 33:10 (NRSV)

- Imagine an authentic situation of conflict, whether interpersonal, intercommunal, or international. What would it look like practically to allow for the full expression of the demands of mercy, truth, justice, and peace in such a contentious situation?

PRAY

Almighty God, our heavenly Father, guide the nations of the world into the way of justice and truth, and establish among them that peace which is the fruit of justice, that they may become the kingdom of our lord and savior Jesus Christ. Amen.

—Adapted from the Book of Common Prayer (1979)

EXPLORE

Lederach, John Paul. *Reconcile: Conflict Transformation for Ordinary Christians.* Harrisonburg: Herald, 2014.

Stassen, Glen H., Rodney L. Peterson, and Timothy A. Norton, eds. *Formation for Life: Just Peacemaking and Twenty-First-Century Discipleship.* Eugene: Pickwick, 2013.

Action Research Associates (https://actionresearchassociates.org/).

38

Empathy Embodied

CENTRAL TO ANY CHRIST-CENTERED EXPLORATION of faith, politics, and the reign of God is the following question: Who, exactly, is my neighbor?

> *One day an expert in religious law stood up to test Jesus by asking him this question: "Teacher, what should I do to inherit eternal life?"*
>
> *Jesus replied, "What does the law of Moses say? How do you read it?"*
>
> *The man answered, "'You must love the Lord your God with all your heart, all your soul, all your strength, and all your mind.' And, 'Love your neighbor as yourself.'"*
>
> *"Right!" Jesus told him. "Do this and you will live!" The man wanted to justify his actions, so he asked Jesus, "And who is my neighbor?"*
>
> *Jesus replied with a story: "A Jewish man was traveling from Jerusalem down to Jericho, and he was attacked by bandits. They stripped him of his clothes, beat him up, and left him half dead beside the road.*
>
> *"By chance a priest came along. But when he saw the man lying there, he crossed to the other side of the road and passed him by. A Temple assistant walked over and looked at him lying there, but he also passed by on the other side.*
>
> *"Then a despised Samaritan came along, and when he saw the man, he felt compassion for him. Going over to him, the Samaritan soothed his wounds with olive oil and wine and bandaged them. Then he put the man on his own donkey and took him to an inn, where he took care of him. The next day he handed the innkeeper two days' wages, telling him, 'Take care of this man. If his bill runs higher than this, I'll pay you the next time I'm here.'*

Serving a Crucified King

> *"Now which of these three would you say was a neighbor to the man who was attacked by bandits?" Jesus asked.*
> *The man replied, "The one who showed him mercy."*
> *Then Jesus said, "Yes, now go and do the same."*
>
> —Luke 10:25–37 (NLT)

Empathy—the ability to envision oneself in the place and circumstances of another (even one's historic "enemies") and then act in response—is essential for any who would follow Jesus. However, it is too often our very religiosity that most stands in the way of lived, practical compassion. Jesus forces us to ask whether we are allowing the things of God to shield us from the heart of God. Do we construct walls of piety between ourselves and others? Yet, the despised Samaritan, the outsider and infidel, acts to save the life of his presumed enemy and does so at great personal risk to himself. Again, we are being forced by Jesus to ask: Whom do we embrace within the reach of our empathy? Importantly, who is being excluded?

Who, exactly, is our neighbor? I think it is clear that Jesus's answer to this question is: everyone! Moreover, as Jesus highlights the faults of his own community while simultaneously applauding the actions of the presumed enemy, this story of the Good Samaritan perfectly illustrates the significance of critical, painful self-examination of one's actions, beliefs, and prejudices. And, it must be stated boldly and without reservation that bigotry has no place within the community of faith. I conclude, therefore, with my favorite words from theologian Miroslav Volf: "As we desire to embrace the other while we remain true to ourselves and to the crucified Messiah, in a sense we already are where we will be when the home of God is established among mortals."[1]

REFLECT

- When in your life have you acted in the same manner as the priest and temple assistant? What factors led you to "pass by on the other side of the road?" Are there specific instances, however, when you have been "the good Samaritan"?

- Are there specific people or people groups that you might have trouble loving, or whom you would consider to be your enemy? What practical steps might be taken to show them unconditional love in the manner of the good Samaritan?

---

1. Volf, *Exclusion and Embrace*, 231.

PRAY

Show me your mercy, O Lord, and gladden my heart. What you see here is a man who has been caught by thieves, wounded and left for dead beside the road. You are the Good Samaritan who picks me up and treats my wounds with your oil and wine. It is your pleasure that I should spend my days in your house with all the others you have gathered there, where I will praise you forever. Amen.

—Jerome of Stridon (fourth century)

EXPLORE

Accad, Martin, and Jonathan Andrews, eds. *The Religious Other: A Biblical Understanding of Islam, the Qur'an, and Muhammad*. Institute of Middle East Studies Series. Carlisle: Langham Global Library, 2020.

Wilson-Hartgrove, Johnathan. *Reconstructing the Gospel: Finding Freedom from Slaveholder Religion*. Downers Grove: IVP Books, 2018.

39

There Are Two Ways

EACH MOMENT OF EACH DAY presents us with a choice as to which king we will follow and in which kingdom we will choose to live.

> So in everything, do to others what you would have them do to you, for this sums up the Law and the Prophets. Enter through the narrow gate. For wide is the gate and broad is the road that leads to destruction, and many enter through it. But small is the gate and narrow the road that leads to life, and only a few find it.
> —MATTHEW 7:12–14 (NIV)

> Not everyone who says to me, "Lord, Lord," will enter the kingdom of heaven, but only the one who does the will of my Father who is in heaven. Many will say to me on that day, "Lord, Lord, did we not prophesy in your name and in your name drive out demons and in your name perform many miracles?" Then I will tell them plainly, "I never knew you. Away from me, you evildoers!"
> —MATTHEW 7:21–23 (NIV)

The Didache, a first-century handbook for new disciples, opens with the following:

> There are two ways, one of life and one of death, but a great difference between the two ways. The way of life, then, is this: First, you shall love God who made you; second, love your neighbor as yourself, and do not do to another what you would not want done to you. And of these sayings the teaching is this: Bless those who curse you, and pray for your enemies, and fast for those who persecute you. For what reward is there for loving those who love

you? Do not the Gentiles do the same? But love those who hate
you, and you shall not have an enemy. Abstain from fleshly and
worldly lusts. If someone strikes your right cheek, turn to him the
other also, and you shall be perfect. If someone impresses you for
one mile, go with him two. If someone takes your cloak, give him
also your coat. If someone takes from you what is yours, ask it not
back, for indeed you are not able. Give to everyone who asks you,
and ask it not back; for the Father wills that to all should be given
of our own blessings.[1]

Again, each moment of each day, each action we take presents us with a choice as to which path we will take, which king we will choose to follow, and in which kingdom we will choose to live here on earth. Key to this determination is continuously asking ourselves the question: In everything, are we doing for others what we would want them to do for us?

REFLECT

- In the past week, when have you intentionally sought to do for others what you would have them do for you? Alternatively, when did you find yourself tempted by the easy path?
- What is the relationship between the Golden Rule and the reign of God?

PRAY

> We ask you, Lord, to be our helper and assister; save those of us who are in affliction; have compassion on the humble; raise the fallen; appear to those who are in need; heal the sinners; convert those of your people who are wandering from the way; feed the hungry; ransom our prisoners; raise up the sick; encourage the feeble-hearted; let all the nations know that you are God alone and Jesus Christ your son, and that we are your people and the sheep of your pasture.
>
> —Clement of Rome (first century)

EXPLORE

Jones, Tony. *The Teaching of the Twelve: Believing & Practicing the Primitive Christianity of the Ancient Didache Community.* Brewster: Paraclete Press, 2009.

---

1. Didache 1:1–5 (Riddle)

40

Worship as Farce

It is a foundational truth of Scripture that a person's value is found in their status as a beloved creation of the Father, purposefully crafted in his image, and as one for whom the son laid down his very own life—not in their capacity to produce or in the price tag of their labor:

> Honor your father and your mother, as the Lord your God has commanded you, so that you may live long and that it may go well with you in the land the Lord your God is giving you.
>
> —Deuteronomy 5:16 (NIV)

> Jesus replied, "You hypocrites! Isaiah was right when he prophesied about you, for he wrote, 'These people honor me with their lips, but their hearts are far from me. Their worship is a farce, for they teach man-made ideas as commands from God.' For you ignore God's law and substitute your own tradition."
>
> Then he said, "You skillfully sidestep God's law in order to hold on to your own tradition. For instance, Moses gave you this law from God: 'Honor your father and mother,' and 'Anyone who speaks disrespectfully of father or mother must be put to death.' But you say it is all right for people to say to their parents, 'Sorry, I can't help you. For I have vowed to give to God what I would have given to you.' In this way, you let them disregard their needy parents. And so you cancel the word of God in order to hand down your own tradition. And this is only one example among many others."
>
> —Mark 7:6–13 (NLT)

It must be remembered that mosaic law was never meant to function as a "checklist for heaven." Rather, it was the means for constructing a new community, a vanguard nation based on the principles of peace, justice, and human dignity, in contrast to the idolatrous and exploitative empires of the day. For this reason, Jesus would one day declare, "I did not come to abolish the law of Moses or the writings of the prophets. No, I came to accomplish their purpose."[1] For the people of his day, as much as our own, would manipulate religion for the purposes of political-economic exploitation. Specifically referencing the command to honor our fathers and mothers, T. Scott Daniels writes,

> The Fifth Commandment is not about obeying parents (although that's what I told my kids). It's a command to protect the elderly even when they can no longer contribute visibly to the economy. How a culture honors the aged and keeps memory is a strong measure of its moral character.[2]

From needing to avoid large gatherings during a global pandemic (during church services for instance) to making humane, age-affirming decisions with regard to elder care, honoring our mothers and fathers is about much more than blind obedience. It's about the moral health of our societies.

REFLECT

- Do you honor your father and mother or those who raised you? What steps can you take this week to show honor to your parents?
- What does it mean to honor our fathers and mothers within a society obsessed with the worship of youth and ephemeral beauty? What practical steps can be taken to honor the fathers and mothers of your community?
- On the other hand, do you have difficulties with this specific teaching? If so, are there practical avenues available to you for authentic healing and reconciliation?

PRAY

> Look with mercy, God our Father, on all whose increasing years bring them weakness, distress, or isolation. Provide for them homes of dignity and peace; give them understanding helpers, and the willingness to accept help; and, as their strength diminishes, increase

---

1. Matthew 5:17 (NLT)
2. Daniels, "Fifth Commandment," Facebook, March 24, 2020.

their faith and their assurance of your love. This we ask in the name of Jesus Christ our Lord. Amen.

—The Book of Common Prayer (1979)

EXPLORE

Daniels, T. Scott. *Embracing Exile: Living Faithfully as God's Unique People in the World.* Kansas City: Nazarene Publishing House, 2017.

Ramachandra, Vinoth. *Subverting Global Myths: Theology and the Public Issues Shaping Our World.* Downers Grove: IVP Academic, 2008.

41

Magic Pools of Water

WITHIN THIS COLLECTION, I HAVE been sharing with you those passages of Scripture that have been most influential in shaping my theo-political outlook. Until very recently, however, I had never considered the sociopolitical implications of the following:

> Inside the city, near the Sheep Gate, was the pool of Bethesda, with five covered porches. Crowds of sick people—blind, lame, or paralyzed—lay on the porches. One of the men lying there had been sick for thirty-eight years. When Jesus saw him and knew he had been ill for a long time, he asked him, "Would you like to get well?"
> "I can't, sir," the sick man said, "for I have no one to put me into the pool when the water bubbles up. Someone else always gets there ahead of me."
> Jesus told him, "Stand up, pick up your mat, and walk!"
> Instantly, the man was healed! He rolled up his sleeping mat and began walking! But this miracle happened on the Sabbath, so the Jewish leaders objected. They said to the man who was cured, "You can't work on the Sabbath! The law doesn't allow you to carry that sleeping mat!"
> —JOHN 5:2–10 (NLT)

When it comes to our initial reading of this passage, we may often find ourselves distracted by what appear to be magic pools of water. What we need to do, however, is focus like Jesus on the paralytic man himself. We need to envision the hopelessness of his situation and imagine ourselves in his place. The emotional poignancy of this story is found in the fact that these pools seem to represent the man's final hope for a cure, quite likely the end of a long and heartbreaking journey. He was found entirely alone, abandoned, left to fend for himself in his disability and his desperation. We must remind ourselves that this may often be what it feels like for our family and friends who suffer from debilitating illnesses and disabilities. Many of whom are forced to navigate a world that is either openly hostile to, exploitative of, or at least not built with their needs in mind. As followers of Jesus, we must always attempt to see things from perspectives not our own, consider the needs of others, and advocate for the full inclusion of everyone at all levels of society. And, just as Jesus first asked the paralytic man if he would like to get well, we must not only allow others speak for themselves but actually listen to their voices and respect their expressed needs when they do.

REFLECT

- Who, in your community, comes to mind as a person suffering because of their disability or debilitating illness? Seek out a conversation with this person and try to understand what specific steps your community could take to include them.

- For those with particular impairments, do you find that your faith community is inclusive and considerate of your needs? What would you like to see from your faith community?

- What actions can you and your faith community take to intentionally include and advocate for all those with special needs in your wider community, region, or nation?

PRAY

We praise you, O God, for our friends, [those who work for the health and well-being of others], who seek the healing of our bodies. We bless you for their gentleness and patience, for their knowledge and skill. We remember the hours of our suffering when they brought relief, and the days of our fear and anguish at the bedside of our dear ones when they came as ministers of God to save the life you have given us. May we reward their fidelity and devotion by our loving gratitude, and uphold them by the satisfaction of work well done. We rejoice in the tireless daring with which some are now tracking the great slayers of humankind by the white light of science. Grant that under their teaching we may grapple with the sins which have ever dealt death to the race, and that we may so order the life of our communities that none may be doomed to an untimely death for lack of the simple gifts which you have given in abundance.

Make our doctors the prophets and soldiers of your kingdom, which is the reign of cleanliness and self-restraint and the dominion of health and joyous life. Strengthen in their whole profession the consciousness that their calling is holy and that they, too, are disciples of the saving Christ. May they never through the pressure of need or ambition surrender the sense of a divine mission and become hirelings who serve only for money. Make them doubly faithful in the service of the poor who need their help most sorely, and may the children of the working man and woman become as precious to them as the child of the rich. Though they deal with the frail body of humans, may they have an abiding sense of the eternal value of the life residing in it, that by call of faith and hope they may summon to their aid the mysterious spirit of humankind and the powers of your all pervading life.

—WALTER RAUSCHENBUSCH (1910)

EXPLORE

Nouwen, Henri J. M. *The Wounded Healer: Ministry in Contemporary Society.* New York: Doubleday, 1979.

42

Bad Theology Kills

IN FOLLOWING THE HEADLINES, WE are shown time and again the simple truth that good theology brings life. And, bad theology kills:

> *Watch out for false prophets. They come to you in sheep's clothing, but inwardly they are ferocious wolves. By their fruit you will recognize them. Do people pick grapes from thornbushes, or figs from thistles? Likewise, every good tree bears good fruit, but a bad tree bears bad fruit. A good tree cannot bear bad fruit, and a bad tree cannot bear good fruit. Every tree that does not bear good fruit is cut down and thrown into the fire. Thus, by their fruit you will recognize them.*
> —MATTHEW 7:15–20 (NIV)

> *A tree is identified by its fruit. If a tree is good, its fruit will be good. If a tree is bad, its fruit will be bad. You brood of snakes! How could evil men like you speak what is good and right? For whatever is in your heart determines what you say. A good person produces good things from the treasury of a good heart, and an evil person produces evil things from the treasury of an evil heart. And I tell you this, you must give an account on judgment day for every idle word you speak. The words you say will either acquit you or condemn you.*
> —MATTHEW 12:33–37 (NLT)

For many, the subject of "theology" invokes the image of old white men with impressive beards and antiquated ideas sitting in ivory seminary towers writing really big books that nobody reads. Yet within everything we think, say, or do can be found a variety of implicit theologies. For theology—alongside its secularized twin, ideology—encompasses our core beliefs as to how the universe functions and how we function within it. It gives shape to our identity and drives our sense of purpose, providing us with the interpretive lenses through which we make sense of and find meaning in our daily lives. In an era of "deconstructed absolutes" and Orwellian doublespeak, when it seems the very concept of truth itself is on trial and public speech has been emptied of substantive content, how is it possible for one to distinguish good theology from bad, or what's true from what is false?

For the follower of Jesus, the answer is surprisingly simple: fruit. To distinguish the true from false prophet, or anyone claiming to represent the will of God, Jesus does not implement a doctrinal litmus test, as crucial as sound doctrine is. Instead, he tells us this: "By their fruit you will recognize them." Too often, however, we find walking the halls of power those false prophets who provide ideological cover for the abuse of power, violent and destructive wars, and the neglect, exploitation, and sacrifice of society's most vulnerable on the altars of profit and politics. Unfortunately, we also find ourselves too often marching along in dutiful compliance, captive to the false allure of destructive ideological systems and their apologists. But, as a popular saying goes, "If your theology doesn't lead you to love people more, you should question your theology." Because distinguishing good theology from bad theology comes down to this: Good theology brings life. Bad theology kills.

REFLECT

Consider the fruit of particular theo-ethical, ideological, or political-economic systems and ask yourself the following:

- Does the historical fruit of these systems lead us to love God, neighbor, and enemy as ourselves? Or, does it result in self-aggrandizement, or separatist and supremacist attitudes?
- Does it seek God's kingdom come and his will be done on earth as it is in heaven? Or, does it seek to promote the dominion of some other "lord"?
- Does it stand up for the poor, the orphan, the widow, and the refugee? Or, does it cause them harm?

PRAY

Almighty and eternal God, so draw our hearts to you, so guide our minds, so fill our imaginations, so control our wills, that we may be wholly yours, utterly dedicated to you; and then use us, we pray, as you will, and always to your glory and the welfare of your people; through our Lord and Savior Jesus Christ. Amen.

—The Book of Common Prayer (1979)

EXPLORE

Walton, Jonathan, Suzie Lahoud, and Sy Hoekstra, eds. *Keeping the Faith: Reflections on Politics & Christianity in the Era of Trump & Beyond.* Middletown: KTF, 2020.

Wheeler, Jesse Steven. "Bad Theology Kills: How We Justify Killing Arabs." *The IMES Blog.* Arab Baptist Theological Seminary (2014). IMES.blog.

43

Worthless Assemblies

THE FIRST CHAPTER OF ISAIAH, the book most quoted by Jesus, contains the following admonition:

> *"The multitude of your sacrifices—what are they to me?" says the Lord. "I have more than enough of burnt offerings, of rams and the fat of fattened animals; I have no pleasure in the blood of bulls and lambs and goats. When you come to appear before me, who has asked this of you, this trampling of my courts? Stop bringing meaningless offerings! Your incense is detestable to me. New Moons, Sabbaths and convocations—I cannot bear your worthless assemblies.*
>
> *"Your New Moon feasts and your appointed festivals I hate with all my being. They have become a burden to me; I am weary of bearing them. When you spread out your hands in prayer, I hide my eyes from you; even when you offer many prayers, I am not listening. Your hands are full of blood! Wash and make yourselves clean. Take your evil deeds out of my sight; stop doing wrong. Learn to do right; seek justice. Defend the oppressed. Take up the cause of the fatherless; plead the case of the widow."*
>
> —ISAIAH 1:11–17 (NIV)

The prophet reminds us once again of that which truly matters to God: those most vulnerable and at risk. Yet, as we continue to spin the wheels of religion, do we ask ourselves what may or may not be of actual importance to God? Do we ever consider to what extent God might even detest our "worthless assemblies," or to what extent it is even possible to love God without adequately loving our neighbor? We assemble for praise, prayer, communion, and the study of Scripture. We tithe, fast, and make sacrifices of our time. All of this is great. But, so long as we ignore injustice and fail in our duty to the vulnerable and oppressed, so long as our "hands are full of blood," our worship services remain little more than empty exercises in futility. As I write these words from home in the midst of a global pandemic, multiple religious leaders throughout my country feign persecution and clamor for the ability to gather together in person, or even do so in a misguided act of lethal defiance. Given the risks posed by such large gatherings to the most vulnerable of our communities, I cannot help but wonder if God would find such assemblages worthless and detestable.

REFLECT

- In your worship, do you and your faith community ask what may or may not be of importance to God? Moreover, to what extent is it even possible to love God without adequately loving our neighbor?
- Is it conceivable that God might detest the religious gatherings of your community? Why? What actions would this require of you?

PRAY

Let us pray together with the psalmist:

> *Arise, Lord! Lift up your hand, O God. Do not forget the helpless. Why does the wicked man revile God? Why does he say to himself, "He won't call me to account"? But you, God, see the trouble of the afflicted; you consider their grief and take it in hand. The victims commit themselves to you; you are the helper of the fatherless. Break the arm of the wicked man; call the evildoer to account for his wickedness that would not otherwise be found out. The Lord is king for ever and ever; the nations will perish from his land. You, Lord, hear the desire of the afflicted; you encourage them, and you listen to their cry, defending the fatherless and the oppressed, so that mere earthly mortals will never again strike terror.*
>
> —Psalm 10:12–18 (NIV)

EXPLORE

Goldingay, John. *The Theology of the Book of Isaiah*. Downers Grove: IVP Academic, 2014.

44

The Great Reversal

THE TEACHINGS OF JESUS ARE often hyper-spiritualized to the point of impotence, if not outright ignored. While this is especially so for the beatitudes of Matthew, doing so becomes significantly more difficult when reading the version presented by Luke:

> He went down with them and stood on a level place. A large crowd of his disciples was there and a great number of people from all over Judea, from Jerusalem, and from the coastal region around Tyre and Sidon, who had come to hear him and to be healed of their diseases. Those troubled by impure spirits were cured, and the people all tried to touch him, because power was coming from him and healing them all. Then he looked up at his disciples and said:
>
> "Blessed are you who are poor, for yours is the kingdom of God. Blessed are you who are hungry now, for you will be filled. Blessed are you who weep now, for you will laugh.
>
> "Blessed are you when people hate you, and when they exclude you, revile you, and defame you on account of the Son of Man. Rejoice in that day and leap for joy, for surely your reward is great in heaven; for that is what their ancestors did to the prophets.
>
> "But woe to you who are rich, for you have received your consolation. Woe to you who are full now, for you will be hungry. Woe to you who are laughing now, for you will mourn and weep. Woe to you when all speak well of you, for that is what their ancestors did to the false prophets."
>
> —LUKE 6:20–26 (NRSV)

The beatitudes, as presented by Luke, are at their core about the powerful and the powerless, "the haves and the have-nots," the in-group and the outcasts, and the great reversal anticipated by God's in-breaking kingdom. Only the most convoluted interpretive gymnastics would allow for a hyper-spiritualized reading of such a direct, real-world admonishment. As disciples, therefore, our social vision must be in alignment with Jesus's radical message if we are to find ourselves standing on "the right side of history," in solidarity with the poor, the hungry, and all those in distress. Also found here is a warning about the authentic persecution we should expect to receive, once we begin to preach and act in ways congruent with the topsy-turvy kingdom of God. For the socio-political and economic implications of God's reign pose a direct challenge to the corrupt, exploitative, and violent kings of this age, alongside those false theo-ethical systems employed in their defense. Luke, it must be said, has bite.

REFLECT

- Take a moment to reread the beatitudes above. Have you heard teachings that seek to hyper-spiritualize the commands of Jesus? If so, write down in your own words exactly what Jesus is telling you to do in this passage.

- What does it mean to speak of the kingdom of God as a "great reversal" or to describe it as "topsy-turvy"? What could a topsy-turvy socio-economic order look like in your specific context?

PRAY

God, we praise you for the dream of the golden city of peace and righteousness which has ever haunted the prophets of humanity, and we rejoice with joy unspeakable that at last the people have conquered the freedom and knowledge and power which may avail to turn into reality the vision that so long has beckoned in vain. Speed now the day when the plains and the hills and the wealth thereof shall be the people's own, and your freemen shall not lie as tenants of men on the earth which you have given to all; when no babe shall be born without its equal birthright in the riches and knowledge wrought out by the labor of the ages; and when the mighty engines of industry shall throb with a gladder music because of the women and men who ply these great tools shall be their owners and masters. Bring to an end, O Lord, the inhumanity of the present, in which all men and women are ridden by the pale fear of want while the nation of which they are citizens sits throned amid the wealth of their making; when the personhood in some is cowed by helplessness, while the soul of others is surfeited and sick with power which no frail child of the dust should wield.

O God, save us, for our nation is at strife with its own soul and is sinning against the light which you aforetime kindled in it. You have called our people to freedom but we are withholding from them their share in the common heritage without which freedom becomes a hollow name. Christ has kindled in us the passion for siblinghood, but the social life we have built, denies and slays siblinghood. We pray for you to revive in us the hardy spirit of our forefathers and mothers that we may establish and complete their work, building on the basis of [their democratic dreams] the firm edifice of a cooperative commonwealth, in which both government and industry shall be of the people, by the people, and for the people. May we, who now live, see the oncoming of the great day of God, when all shall stand side by side in equal worth and real freedom, all toiling and all reaping, masters of nature but brothers and sisters of humankind, exultant in the tide of the common life, and jubilant in the adoration of you, the source of their blessings and the Father of all.

—Walter Rauschenbusch (1910)

EXPLORE

Brueggemann, Walter. *Materiality as Resistance: Five Elements for Moral Action in the Real World.* Louisville: Westminster John Knox Press, 2020.

45

Willing to Listen

WE CONTINUE TODAY IN JESUS'S Sermon on the Plain found in Luke's gospel. I can only imagine how our world might look if the approximately 2.4 billion confessed Christians living in the world today—nearly thirty percent of the global population—were to truly listen to these words and put them into practice. For these words are socially and culturally transformative. They were meant to be taken seriously, and they were meant to be enacted.

> *But to you who are willing to listen, I say, love your enemies! Do good to those who hate you. Bless those who curse you. Pray for those who hurt you. If someone slaps you on one cheek, offer the other cheek also. If someone demands your coat, offer your shirt also. Give to anyone who asks; and when things are taken away from you, don't try to get them back. Do to others as you would like them to do to you.*
>
> *If you love only those who love you, why should you get credit for that? Even sinners love those who love them! And if you do good only to those who do good to you, why should you get credit? Even sinners do that much! And, if you lend money only to those who can repay you, why should you get credit? Even sinners will lend to other sinners for a full return.*
>
> *Love your enemies! Do good to them. Lend to them without expecting to be repaid. Then your reward from heaven will be very great, and you will truly be acting as children of the Most High, for he is kind to those who are unthankful and wicked. You must be compassionate, just as your Father is compassionate.*
>
> *Do not judge others, and you will not be judged. Do not condemn others, or it will all come back against you. Forgive others,*

Willing to Listen

and you will be forgiven. Give, and you will receive. Your gift will return to you in full—pressed down, shaken together to make room for more, running over, and poured into your lap. The amount you give will determine the amount you get back.

Then Jesus gave the following illustration: Can one blind person lead another? Won't they both fall into a ditch? Students are not greater than their teacher. But the student who is fully trained will become like the teacher.

And why worry about a speck in your friend's eye when you have a log in your own? How can you think of saying, "Friend, let me help you get rid of that speck in your eye," when you can't see past the log in your own eye? Hypocrite! First get rid of the log in your own eye; then you will see well enough to deal with the speck in your friend's eye

A good tree can't produce bad fruit, and a bad tree can't produce good fruit. A tree is identified by its fruit. Figs are never gathered from thornbushes, and grapes are not picked from bramble bushes. A good person produces good things from the treasury of a good heart, and an evil person produces evil things from the treasury of an evil heart. What you say flows from what is in your heart.

So why do you keep calling me "Lord, Lord!" when you don't do what I say? I will show you what it's like when someone comes to me, listens to my teaching, and then follows it. It is like a person building a house who digs deep and lays the foundation on solid rock. When the floodwaters rise and break against that house, it stands firm because it is well built. But anyone who hears and doesn't obey is like a person who builds a house right on the ground, without a foundation. When the floods sweep down against that house, it will collapse into a heap of ruins.

—Luke 6:27–49 (NLT)

REFLECT

Rather than comment on today's passage, I ask you to sit with it for a few minutes in silence. Reflect upon the transformative power contained within these words of Jesus, provided we are not only willing to listen but also enact them in our daily lives.

PRAY

Then, slowly read through the passage again, focusing on the section that convicts you the most or upon the concept you find most troubling. Pray over it. Ask the Lord to guide and direct you with regard to how he might be speaking through it to you at this moment. Ask for guidance and direction as to how you might be able to not only hear these words but put them into practice in your daily life.

EXPLORE

Boyle, Gregory. *Tattoos on the Heart: The Power of Boundless Compassion.* New York: Free Press, 2011.

46

#FarTooManyMen

MORE THAN A WARNING AGAINST self-righteous judgmentalism, of which we are so often guilty, the following passage serves as a forceful condemnation of the violence inherent to the patriarchal worldview that defines so many of our communities:

> Then early the next morning he went to the temple. The people came to him, and he sat down and started teaching them. The Pharisees and the teachers of the Law of Moses brought in a woman who had been caught in bed with a man who wasn't her husband. They made her stand in the middle of the crowd.
> Then they said, "Teacher, this woman was caught sleeping with a man who isn't her husband. The Law of Moses teaches that a woman like this should be stoned to death! What do you say?"
> They asked Jesus this question, because they wanted to test him and bring some charge against him. But Jesus simply bent over and started writing on the ground with his finger.
> They kept on asking Jesus about the woman. Finally, he stood up and said, "If any of you have never sinned, then go ahead and throw the first stone at her!"
> Once again he bent over and began writing on the ground. The people left one by one, beginning with the oldest. Finally, Jesus and the woman were there alone. Jesus stood up and asked her, "Where is everyone? Isn't there anyone left to accuse you?"
> "No sir," the woman answered.
> Then Jesus told her, "I am not going to accuse you either. You may go now, but don't sin anymore."
>
> —JOHN 8:2–11 (CEV)

We must first ask ourselves: if she was caught in the act, then where is the man? Why, in America as much as the Middle East and elsewhere, is it that only women are forced to bear upon their bodies the weight of social morality, status, and shame? In bending down to write in the dirt, the actual content of which we will never know, Jesus is intentionally removing the eyes of scorn away from the woman and refocusing them upon himself. History reveals that the rotten fruit of patriarchy is abuse, as women and girls are crushed beneath the wheels of male privilege. Too often, men with power use that power to extract what they want from women while perpetuating a culture of shame and dependence. Operating beneath a veneer of respectable religiosity, they enforce a culture of silence upon the threat of exclusion, poverty, violence, or even death. Yet, time and again, the gospels subvert gender expectations to unequivocally affirm the dignity and equality of women. Jesus effectively broke the law in service to the greater righteousness.

REFLECT

- Where do you imagine the man was while his lover was publicly condemned and brought to shame before the eyes of the watching community? Putting yourself in the man's place, what could you have done differently to effect truth and justice in this situation?

- Identify an instance where you have seen a woman (or women) crushed beneath the violent wheels of patriarchy? What harmful, patriarchal practices have you justified? What can you do now to make that right?

PRAY

Lord Jesus Christ, Son of God, have mercy on me, a sinner.
—The Jesus Prayer (traditional)

EXPLORE

Buttry, Sharon A., and Dan L. Buttry. *Daughters of Rizpah: Nonviolence and the Transformation of Trauma.* Eugene: Cascade Books, 2020.

47

A Good Man

Seen from the male perspective in the book of Matthew (as opposed to the female perspective presented by Luke) this is the story of Joseph the Just:

> This is how Jesus Christ was born: His mother Mary was engaged to Joseph, but, before the marriage took place, she found herself to be pregnant by the power of the Holy Spirit. Her husband, Joseph, was a just man and, since he did not want to disgrace her publicly, he resolved to put an end to their engagement privately. He had been [fuming over this],[1] when an angel of the Lord appeared to him in a dream.
>
> "Joseph, son of David," the angel said, "do not be afraid to take Mary for your wife, for her child has been conceived by the power of the Holy Spirit. She will give birth to a son; name him Jesus, for he will save his people from their sins."
>
> All this happened in fulfillment of these words of the Lord through the prophet, where he says—"The virgin will conceive and will give birth to a son, and they will give him the name Immanuel"— a word which means "God is with us." When Joseph woke up, he did as the angel of the Lord had directed him. He made Mary his wife, but they did not sleep together before the birth of her son; and to this son he gave the name Jesus.
>
> —Matthew 1:18–21 (OEB)

This is a powerful story, bubbling just below the surface with incredible meaning. In his day, Joseph had every legal, religious, and social

---

1. Bailey, *Middle Eastern Eyes*, 45.

right—perhaps obligation!—to seek Mary's public humiliation and execution. This is a world of honor killings, where any hint of sexual impropriety on behalf of a young woman could result in either her social banishment or death at the hands of those closest to her. In fact, such consequences were enshrined in religious law. As such, this represents yet an additional instance whereby women and girls are found crushed beneath the wheels of religiously-sanctioned patriarchy.

In the version presented by Luke, we find Mary willingly taking upon herself such a risk for the sake of the world's salvation. In Matthew, as New Testament scholar Kenneth Bailey informs us, we find a just man who set aside his justified anger to break both law and custom for the sake of the greater righteousness[2]—prophetically defined as compassion for the vulnerable. This, he did prior to any divine intervention. What we find in this story, therefore, is an unequivocal affirmation and celebration of life as the sign of God's blessing, regardless of the circumstances by which that new life is conceived. This is a bold rejection of those death-dealing laws, customs, and belief systems that would seek to extinguish the life of a mother and her child. From this story comes the world's salvation.

REFLECT

- Imagine yourself in the position of Joseph. How would you respond to the news that your betrothed was found pregnant by someone other than yourself? What might this story teach us about listening to and respecting the voice and rights of women?

- At what times may it be appropriate, even necessary, "to break the law for the sake of a greater good?" When would it be inappropriate to do so?

PRAY

Lord God, grant us the wisdom and courage to learn from and follow Joseph's example, a judicious willingness to defy both law and custom for the sake of a greater, life-affirming holiness. Open our eyes and our hearts to the experiences, insecurities, and hardship of others, that we might become agents of your divine grace, love, and deliverance for those you have placed in our life. Guide us in the path of true righteousness and restorative justice, even at the expense of

---

2. Bailey, *Middle Eastern Eyes*, 43–47.

our pride and public image. We pray this in your holy name Lord Jesus. Amen.

—A Prayer for Wisdom and Courage (original)

EXPLORE

DeSilva, David A. *Honor, Patronage, Kinship & Purity: Unlocking New Testament Culture.* Downers Grove: IVP Academic, 2012.

McCullough, Andy. *The Bethlehem Story: Mission and Justice in the Margins of the World.* Eugene: Resource, 2021.

48

Mary Knew

THIS IS THE STORY OF Mary, the intrepid young woman who upon being presented with an otherwise impossible situation as an unmarried first-century teen chose to risk everything for the sake of God's reign and the world's salvation. As you read, imagine yourself in the place and circumstances of young Mary:

> *In the sixth month of Elizabeth's pregnancy, God sent the angel Gabriel to Nazareth, a town in Galilee, to a virgin pledged to be married to a man named Joseph, a descendant of David. The virgin's name was Mary. The angel went to her and said, "Greetings, you who are highly favored! The Lord is with you."*
>
> *Mary was greatly troubled at his words and wondered what kind of greeting this might be. But the angel said to her, "Do not be afraid, Mary; you have found favor with God. You will conceive and give birth to a son, and you are to call him Jesus. He will be great and will be called the Son of the Most High. The Lord God will give him the throne of his father David, and he will reign over Jacob's descendants forever; his kingdom will never end."*
>
> *"How will this be," Mary asked the angel, "since I am a virgin?"*
>
> *The angel answered, "The Holy Spirit will come on you, and the power of the Most High will overshadow you. So the holy one to be born will be called the Son of God. Even Elizabeth your relative is going to have a child in her old age, and she who was said to be unable to conceive is in her sixth month. For no word from God will ever fail."*
>
> *"I am the Lord's servant," Mary answered. "May your word to me be fulfilled." Then the angel left her.*

Mary Knew

> *At that time Mary got ready and hurried to a town in the hill country of Judea, where she entered Zechariah's home and greeted Elizabeth. When Elizabeth heard Mary's greeting, the baby leaped in her womb, and Elizabeth was filled with the Holy Spirit. In a loud voice she exclaimed: "Blessed are you among women, and blessed is the child you will bear! But why am I so favored, that the mother of my Lord should come to me? As soon as the sound of your greeting reached my ears, the baby in my womb leaped for joy. Blessed is she who has believed that the Lord would fulfill his promises to her!"*
>
> —Luke 1:26–45 (NIV)

Joseph had no reason to seek Mary's well-being and in fact had every legal and socio-cultural obligation to pursue its opposite. Nevertheless, Mary chose to walk valiantly through the valley of the shadow of death, in faithful anticipation of her son's own sacrifice. She had faith, like Abraham before her, that the child of promise would survive. So, taking upon herself and embracing the shame that could have so easily extinguished the light she carried within her, Mary would eventually become the most honored woman of history. Though she fled Nazareth for the Judean highlands, Mary found herself surrounded not by those who would condemn her for a presumed promiscuity but by those who recognized within her the divine presence on earth and loved her accordingly. I think it is fair to say that this must also be our example, to recognize the presence of the divine within everyone we encounter and respond accordingly—most especially those young women and men who find themselves caught-up in extraordinary circumstances. Finally, recognizing Mary's virginity must never result in an ultimately unhealthy idolization of celibacy or ascetic excess that merely perpetuates the culture of shame, patriarchy, and hyper-spiritualism being subverted by the incarnation story.

REFLECT

- In art and literature, Mary is depicted often as a meek and ultimately passive participant in the divine plan, an empty vessel so to speak. How might thinking of her instead as a proactive, selfless actor in the Christmas story impact your understanding of the incarnation?
- In what ways have you or your faith community allowed a sense of purity, moralism, or traditional religiosity to negatively impact the most vulnerable members of your community?

PRAY

With Mary, let us glorify the Lord:

> *With all my heart I glorify the Lord! In the depths of who I am I rejoice in God my savior. He has looked with favor on the low status of his servant. Look! From now on, everyone will consider me highly favored because the mighty one has done great things for me. Holy is his name. He shows mercy to everyone, from one generation to the next, who honors him as God. He has shown strength with his arm. He has scattered those with arrogant thoughts and proud inclinations. He has pulled the powerful down from their thrones and lifted up the lowly. He has filled the hungry with good things and sent the rich away empty-handed. He has come to the aid of his servant Israel, remembering his mercy, just as he promised to our ancestors, to Abraham and to Abraham's descendants forever.*
>
> —The Magnificat (Luke 1:46–55, CEB)

EXPLORE

Miller, Brandi. *Advent*. Seattle: Reclaiming My Theology, 2020.

Tucker, Ruth A., and Walter Liefeld. *Daughters of the Church: Women and Ministry from New Testament Times to the Present*. Grand Rapids: Zondervan, 1987.

49

The Root of Jesse

JESSE, A SHEPHERD FROM BETHLEHEM, was the father of King David, grandfather to Solomon, progenitor of the Judean dynasty, and a direct ancestor of Joseph. In the words of Isaiah, he becomes representative of the messianic line cut down during the Babylonian conquest and subsequent exile. Here, the prophet envisions the return of the messianic king as the very coming of God himself:

> Out of the stump of Jesse will grow a shoot—yes, a new Branch bearing fruit from the old root. And the Spirit of the Lord will rest on him—the Spirit of wisdom and understanding, the Spirit of counsel and might, the Spirit of knowledge and the fear of the Lord. He will delight in obeying the Lord. He will not judge by appearance nor make a decision based on hearsay. He will give justice to the poor and make fair decisions for the exploited. The earth will shake at the force of his word, and one breath from his mouth will destroy the wicked. He will wear righteousness like a belt and truth like an undergarment.
>
> In that day the wolf and the lamb will live together; the leopard will lie down with the baby goat. The calf and the yearling will be safe with the lion, and a little child will lead them all. The cow will graze near the bear. The cub and the calf will lie down together. The lion will eat hay like a cow. The baby will play safely near the hole of a cobra. Yes, a little child will put its hand in a nest of deadly snakes without harm. Nothing will hurt or destroy in all my holy mountain, for as the waters fill the sea, so the earth will be filled with people who know the Lord. In that day the root of Jesse will be a banner of salvation to all the world.

Serving a Crucified King

—Isaiah 11:1–10 (NLT)

In the striking imagery of the ancient Near East, Isaiah presents us with a messianic vision of God's future reign, a vision of cosmic reconciliation between God, humanity, and all creation wherein the powerful no longer feast upon the weak and vulnerable. To the followers of Jesus, this reign was first inaugurated in Christ, yet is to be fully realized upon his return. In the meantime, however, our collective task as the body of Christ (empowered by the Holy Spirit of God's presence among us) is to do all we can to see our present, earthly reality defined by this future vision of peace, justice, and joy. The king's mission becomes our mission. For "in that day, the root of Jesse will be a banner of salvation to the world."

REFLECT

- Does your vision of the future include within it the establishment of a just peace here on earth?
- Taking Isaiah's vision as your guide, how would you rewrite your faith community's approach to mission and ministry in your neighborhood or region?

PRAY

Together with the prophet, we pray:

> *Our Lord, you always do right, and you make the path smooth for those who obey you. You are the one we trust to bring about justice; above all else we want your name to be honored. Throughout the night, my heart searches for you, because your decisions show everyone on this earth how to live right . . . You will give us peace, Lord, because everything we have done was by your power. Others have ruled over us besides you, our Lord God, but we obey only you.*
>
> —Isaiah 26:7–9; 12–13 (CEV)

EXPLORE

Wright, Christopher J. H. *The Mission of God: Unlocking the Bible's Grand Narrative.* Downers Grove: IVP Academic, 2013.

50

Into Practice

THROUGHOUT THIS COLLECTION, I HAVE been sharing those passages of Scripture most instrumental in my own attempts at traversing the dangerous waters of faith and politics—those most influential in giving shape to my theo-political outlook. Central to this outlook is the conviction that Jesus Christ is to be followed, as king! His divine words are to be lived out in practice, not simply believed. As Jesus warns us in his conclusion to the Sermon on the Mount:

> *Not everyone who says to me, "Lord, Lord," will enter the kingdom of heaven, but only the one who does the will of my Father who is in heaven. Many will say to me on that day, "Lord, Lord, did we not prophesy in your name and in your name drive out demons and in your name perform many miracles?" Then I will tell them plainly, "I never knew you. Away from me, you evildoers!"*
>
> *Therefore everyone who hears these words of mine and puts them into practice is like a wise man who built his house on the rock. The rain came down, the streams rose, and the winds blew and beat against that house; yet it did not fall, because it had its foundation on the rock. But everyone who hears these words of mine and does not put them into practice is like a foolish man who built his house on sand. The rain came down, the streams rose, and the winds blew and beat against that house, and it fell with a great crash.*
>
> —MATTHEW 7:21–27 (NIV)

Dietrich Bonhoeffer was a German pastor and theologian tragically martyred for his public opposition to Hitler and the Nazi regime. Famously, he spoke of "cheap grace," a concept defined as "the preaching of forgiveness without requiring repentance, baptism without church discipline. Communion without confession."[1] It is faith without deeds, discipleship without the red letters of Jesus, and kingdom without the cross. In his day, this notion of salvation without sacrifice rendered the church susceptible to and captive of the demonic enchantments of Nazi and other fascistic ideologies. Today, I fear we are at an equally dangerous moment concerning the Christian church's ideological captivity to the false, corrupt, and violent kings of this age. In what are among the most personally transformative paragraphs I have ever read, Christian ethicists Glen Stassen and David Gushee write,

> Christianity is a nonsensical enterprise apart from Jesus, its central figure, its source, ground, authority, and destiny.
>
> Christian churches across the theological and confessional spectrum . . . are often guilty of evading Jesus, the cornerstone and center of the Christian faith. Specifically, *the teachings and practices of Jesus*—especially the largest block of his teaching, the Sermon on the Mount—are routinely ignored or misinterpreted in the preaching and teaching ministry of the churches . . . This evasion of the concrete ethical teachings of Jesus has seriously malformed Christian moral practices, moral beliefs, and moral witness. Jesus taught that the test of our discipleship is whether we act on his teachings, whether we "put into practice" his words. This is what it means to "buil[d our] house on rock."
>
> We believe Jesus meant what he said. And so it is no overstatement to claim that the evasion of the teachings of Jesus constitutes a crisis of Christian identity and raises the question of who exactly is functioning as the Lord of the church. When Jesus's way of discipleship is thinned down, marginalized, or avoided, then churches and Christians lose their antibodies against infection by secular ideologies that manipulate Christians into serving the purposes of some other lord. We fear precisely that kind of idolatry now.[2]

As long as the contemporary church continues to act in a manner so seemingly at odds with the mission and message of Jesus, it remains in a state of crisis. Albeit a serious charge, solving this crisis is of the utmost importance if we are to live once again in faithful obedience to Jesus Christ, as king. For the magnitude of the problem necessitates the establishment of a movement of kingdom citizens devoted to the cruciform reign of Christ and committed to a wholesale transformation in thinking and practice within the church.

1. Bonhoeffer, *Discipleship*, 44.
2. Stassen and Gushee, *Kingdom Ethics*, xvi.

Into Practice

REFLECT

- To what extent do you or your faith community intentionally put into practice the concrete ethical teachings of Jesus as presented in the gospels?
- Who, or what, competes with Jesus Christ for your allegiance as lord of your life, the church, and your wider socio-cultural context?

PRAY

Blessed are all your beloved, my God and King, who have travelled over the tempestuous sea of mortality, and have at last made the desired port of peace and felicity. Cast a gracious eye upon us who are still in our dangerous voyage. Remember and comfort us in our distress, and consider those that lie exposed to the rough storms of hardship and temptation. Strengthen our weakness, that we may do valiantly in this spiritual war; help us against our own negligence and cowardice, and defend us from the treachery of our unfaithful hearts. We are exceedingly frail, and disinclined to every virtuous and noble undertaking. Grant, O Lord, that we may bring our vessel safe to shore, unto our desired haven. Amen.

—Augustine of Hippo (fifth century)

EXPLORE

Gushee, David P., and Glen H. Stassen. *Kingdom Ethics: Following Jesus in Contemporary Context*. Second Edition. Grand Rapids: Eerdmans, 2016.

Palm Sunday

The Triumphal Entry

Though not always acknowledged, Holy Week is brimming with theo-political significance. Simply consider the subversive brilliance of the events in the following passage, when contrasted with the opulent, militaristic splendor of an imperial parade (or *triumphus*) for a returning or conquering king. In this act, surrounded by the poor of the land, Jesus represents in every way the antithesis of Caesar and his modern equivalents:

> *When Jesus and his disciples came near Jerusalem, he went to Bethphage on the Mount of Olives and sent two of them on ahead. He told them, "Go into the next village, where you will at once find a donkey and her colt. Untie the two donkeys and bring them to me. If anyone asks why you are doing that, just say, 'The Lord needs them.' Right away he will let you have the donkeys."*
>
> *So God's promise came true, just as the prophet had said, "Announce to the people of Jerusalem: 'Your king is coming to you! He is humble and rides on a donkey. He comes on the colt of a donkey.'" The disciples left and did what Jesus had told them to do. They brought the donkey and its colt and laid some clothes on their backs. Then Jesus got on.*
>
> *Many people spread clothes in the road, while others put down branches which they had cut from trees. Some people walked ahead of Jesus and others followed behind. They were all shouting, "Hooray for the Son of David! God bless the one who comes in the name of the Lord. Hooray for God in heaven above!" When Jesus came to Jerusalem, everyone in the city was excited and asked, "Who can this be?" The crowd answered, "This is Jesus, the prophet from Nazareth in Galilee."*

The Triumphal Entry

—Matthew 21:1–11 (CEV)

Everyone in Jerusalem, celebrate and shout! Your king has won a victory, and he is coming to you. He is humble and rides on a donkey; he comes on the colt of a donkey. I, the Lord, will take away war chariots and horses from Israel and Jerusalem. Bows that were made for battle will be broken. I will bring peace to nations, and your king will rule from sea to sea. His kingdom will reach from the Euphrates River across the earth.

—Zechariah 9:9–10 (CEV)

When Jesus came closer and could see Jerusalem, he cried and said: It is too bad that today your people don't know what will bring them peace! Now it is hidden from them. Jerusalem, the time will come when your enemies will build walls around you to attack you. Armies will surround you and close in on you from every side. They will level you to the ground and kill your people. Not one stone in your buildings will be left on top of another. This will happen because you did not see that God had come to save you.

—Luke 19:41–44 (CEV)

Through enacted parody, Jesus excoriates the Roman imperial machine and makes a mockery of those who would pursue political and religious status by means of violent conquest. As N. T. Wright tells us, "This is a very carefully staged piece of theologically motivated street theatre. And it works like that. And Jesus knew exactly what buttons he was pressing and what was going to happen."[1] The Roman *triumphus*, upon which later royal and military processions are based, was a sign and celebration of imperial religion whereby a general or emperor would receive public adulation and divine blessing in response to a recent military victory. The returning king, in symbolic purple dress emphasizing his near-divine status, would parade through the city as a conquering hero ahead of his army and with an opulent display of foreign captives and the treasures of war.

This public spectacle would culminate in a consecration ceremony at the Temple of Jupiter Capitolinus, the empire's most sacred temple. As immortalized on the Arch of Titus standing in Rome to this day, just such an event occurred after the Roman armies laid waste to Jerusalem and the temple in 70 AD in retaliation for the Jewish uprising. This parade featured

---

1. Wright, "A Conversation," https://www.patheos.com/blogs/jesuscreed/2019/04/18/two-enacted-parables-rjs/.

700 captive Judeans, the Menorah and the "Table of the Bread of God's Presence," and public executions. Failing to heed the words of the prophet and falling victim to the seductive allure of armed struggle (the very tool of empire), the Judeans failed to recognize "that which would make for peace," the way of cruciform sacrifice. And, it would bring down the full wrath of Roman imperial might upon their city, their temple, and their entire way of life—an act of destruction from which they would ultimately never recover.

REFLECT

- How does a knowledge of the Roman imperial context impact your understanding of Palm Sunday? What light might such an historical understanding shed on the events of Good Friday and Easter?

- Consider your own socio-cultural context. In what ways do you find religion being employed in the service of the powers that be and/or violent conflict?

PRAY

With the Psalmist, let us proclaim:

> *I will give you thanks, for you answered me; you have become my salvation. The stone the builders rejected has become the cornerstone; the Lord has done this, and it is marvelous in our eyes. The Lord has done it this very day; let us rejoice today and be glad.*
>
> *Lord, save us! Lord, grant us success! Blessed is he who comes in the name of the Lord. From the house of the Lord we bless you.*
>
> *The Lord is God, and he has made his light shine on us. With boughs in hand, join in the festal procession up to the horns of the altar. You are my God, and I will praise you; you are my God, and I will exalt you. Give thanks to the Lord, for he is good; his love endures forever.*
>
> —PSALM 118:21–29 (NIV)

EXPLORE

Bruce, F. F. *New Testament Development of Old Testament Themes*. Milton Keynes: Paternoster Press, 1968.

Holy Monday

Overturning Tables

ECHOING THE ROMAN *TRIUMPHUS*, JESUS concludes his triumphal march at the Jerusalem Temple. But, rather than perpetuate the propagandistic cult of imperial religion, Jesus undertakes an act of prophetic brilliance, essentially engineered to incur the wrath of the exploitative religio-political and economic powers of the city:

> *On reaching Jerusalem, Jesus entered the temple courts and began driving out those who were buying and selling there. He overturned the tables of the money changers and the benches of those selling doves, and would not allow anyone to carry merchandise through the temple courts. And as he taught them, he said, "Is it not written: 'My house will be called a house of prayer for all nations'? But you have made it 'a den of robbers.'"*
>
> *The chief priests and the teachers of the law heard this and began looking for a way to kill him, for they feared him, because the whole crowd was amazed at his teaching.*
>
> —MARK 11:15–18 (NIV)

> *Improve your conduct and your actions, and I will dwell with you in this place. Don't trust in lies: "This is the Lord's temple! The Lord's temple! The Lord's temple!" No, if you truly reform your ways and your actions; if you treat each other justly; if you stop taking advantage of the immigrant, orphan, or widow; if you don't shed the blood of the innocent in this place, or go after other gods to your own ruin, only then will I dwell with you in this place . . .*
>
> *Will you steal and murder, commit adultery and perjury, sacrifice to Baal and go after other gods that you don't know, and then*

> *come and stand before me in this temple that bears my name, and say, "We are safe," only to keep on doing all these detestable things? Do you regard this temple, which bears my name, as a hiding place for criminals?*
>
> —Jeremiah 7:3–11 (CEB)

In the temple, Jesus rages against the corruption of religious practice for the sake of financial gain. But, historical context is key. In early Jewish thought, the temple existed as the center of the cosmos. It housed the very presence, or *shekinah*, of God, served as the place of meeting between God and humankind, and acted as the singular point at which heaven and earth overlap. During the post-exilic era of the Second Temple, however, it also acted as the center of Judean political-economic life, with high priests essentially functioning as theocrats (pre-Herod) or Roman imperial puppets (post-Herod).

Furthermore, Hellenistic temples functioned as regional economic exchanges, as banks wherein debts were recorded. They were the financial centers through which the extractive imperial economy operated, and the Jerusalem Temple at this time was no different.[1] It was simply too much, therefore, that the Lord's own house had become the very source of the people's exploitation, poverty, and debt—the result of an unholy amalgamation of wealth, power, and piety. In response, we find Jesus, the living temple in whose person is found the presence (*shekinah*) of God on earth, standing outside of and in judgment against the very edifice constructed to house that presence.[2] Ultimately, Jesus constituted an existential threat to the status quo, and it would cost him his life.

REFLECT

- How do contemporary religio-political and economic entanglements resemble those of the ancient temple? In what ways do our modern realities differ?

- Budgets reflect our moral and ethical priorities. How does Jesus function as Lord over your financial decision making? How might this change your personal or family budget? Consider also your community of faith, workplace, or local and regional government.

---

1. Hudson, *Debts*, 226–227.
2. Wright, *Simply Jesus*, 129–135.

PRAY

We cry to you for justice, O Lord, for our soul is weary with the iniquity of greed. Behold the servants of Mammon, who defy you and drain their fellow men and women for gain; who grind down the strength of workers by merciless toil and fling them aside when they are mangled and worn; who ransack the poor and make dear the space and air which you have made free; who paralyze the hand of justice by corruption and blind the eyes of the people by lies; who nullify by their craft the merciful laws which nobler men have devised for the protection of the weak; who have made us ashamed of our dear country by their defilements and have turned our holy freedom into a hollow name; who have brought upon your church the contempt of humanity and have cloaked their extortion with the gospel of Christ.

For the oppression of the poor and the sighing of the needy now do you arise, O Lord; for because you are love, and tender as a mother to the weak, therefore, you are the great hater of iniquity and your doom is upon those who grow rich on the poverty of the people. Oh God, we are afraid, for the thundercloud of your wrath is even now black above us. In the ruins of dead empires we have read how you have trodden the wine-press of your anger when the measure of their sin was full. We are sick at heart when we remember that by the greed of those who enslaved another race that curse was fastened upon us all which still lies black and hopeless across our land, though the blood of a nation was spilled to atone. Save our people from being dragged down into vaster guilt and woe by those who have no vision and know no law except their lust. Shake their souls with awe of you that they may cease. Help us with clean hands to tear the web which they have woven about us and turn our people back to your law, lest the mark of beast stand out on the right hand and forehead of our nation and our feet be set on the downward path of darkness from which there is no return forever.

—WALTER RAUSCHENBUSCH (1910)

EXPLORE

Hudson, Michael. . . . *and forgive them their debts: Lending, Foreclosure and Redemption from Bronze Age Finance to the Jubilee Year.* Dresden: ISLET-Verlag, 2018.

Holy Tuesday

What Belongs to God

ONCE AGAIN, HOLY WEEK BRIMS with theo-political significance. As such, file the following under "the passage doesn't mean what we often think it means."

> *The legal experts and chief priests were watching Jesus closely and sent spies who pretended to be sincere. They wanted to trap him in his words so they could hand him over to the jurisdiction and authority of the governor. They asked him, "Teacher, we know that you are correct in what you say and teach. You don't show favoritism but teach God's way as it really is. Does the Law allow people to pay taxes to Caesar or not?"*
>
> *Since Jesus recognized their deception, he said to them, "Show me a coin. Whose image and inscription does it have on it?"*
>
> *"Caesar's," they replied.*
>
> *He said to them, "Give to Caesar what belongs to Caesar and to God what belongs to God."*
>
> *They couldn't trap him in his words in front of the people. Astonished by his answer, they were speechless.*
>
> —LUKE 20:20–26 (CEB)

Too often this passage has been used to promote a particular kind of sacred versus secular dualism, such that even if God remains "lord of our souls," it is nevertheless Caesar who reigns over everything else. Yet, these hyper-spiritualized views result in a dualism that the biblical authors would never recognize. This dualism effectively defangs the prophetic witness, fashioning a lord other than God to rule over our socio-political and financial lives. It displaces the very lordship of God being asserted in this moment by

Jesus. But, the creator of the universe does not reside in a spiritual box. For instance, the phrase, "Give to Caesar what belongs to Caesar and to God what belongs to God," immediately begs the question: What doesn't belong to God? As paraphrased by Glen Stassen and David Gushee, "The second member of the parallelism . . . means 'render everything to God.' It gives an ironic twist to the first half of the teaching: God has sovereignty over Caesar; we render to Caesar only what fits God's will."[1]

This is especially so as it relates to questions of our ultimate allegiance and upon whose altar we lay down our time, our resources, or even our very lives. New Testament scholar Donald Hagner comments, "We must render to God our very selves in obedience and service, which will in time touch all we have and own. Caesar can have his paltry tax if only one gives to God his due."[2] For as Jesus tells us, "No one can serve two masters."[3] So, within the politically charged atmosphere of the imperial occupation (soon to erupt in open warfare), the question of taxation was used to differentiate between rebel and collaborator. The religious leaders were attempting to trick Jesus into speaking open treason or blasphemy. Instead, Jesus turns the question back on them by highlighting their own complicity in the exploitative imperial system—holding as they were in the midst of the temple courtyard the "graven image of a self-proclaimed god."[4] Ultimately, the way of Jesus is neither revolution nor collaboration. It is both wholly just and nonviolent.

REFLECT

- What does it mean to conduct your affairs in light of the reality that *all things* belong to God? Look around the room or place you sit now. Say to yourself "this belongs to God" about everything you touch today.

- What would a commitment to justice on the one hand and nonviolence on the other look like in practice? Think of one step you can take this week that reflects Jesus's concern for justice and non-violence.

---

1. Stassen and Gushee, *Kingdom Ethics*, 90.
2. Hagner, *Matthew 14–28*, 636.
3. Matthew 6:24 (NRSV)
4. Wright, *God became King*, 149–150; Stassen and Gushee, *Kingdom Ethics*, 88–92.

PRAY

God, we worship you as the sole lord and sovereign of humanity, and render free obedience to you because your laws are just and your will is love. We pray to you for the kings and princes of the nations to whom power has descended from the past, and for the lords of industry and trade in whose hands the wealth and power of our modern world have gathered. We beseech you to save them from the terrible temptations of their position, lest they follow in the somber lineage of those who have lorded in the past and have used the people's powers for their oppression. Suffer them not to waste the labor of the many for their own luxury, or to use the precious life-blood of men and women for the corruption of all.

Open their hearts to the saving spirit of a new age of freedom. Mature in their souls the unshakable conviction that all they have is but held in trust for a time till the heir shall claim his own. And when the people seek the ampler freedom and self-direction of personhood, may there be no blindness to the higher will and no hardening of heart by those who have ruled. Grant them wisdom so large-hearted that they may recognize the culmination of their task in yielding up their powers, and may use their gathered knowledge in guiding the liberation of the people in order and stability. Save them from the fear and hate which are the tyrants' portion and from the scorn of coming generations. Reveal to them that all the higher joys come only by imparting the strength of our life to those who need it, and that a person's life consists not in the things possessed, but in the love that flows out from them and flows back to them.

—WALTER RAUSCHENBUSCH (1910)

EXPLORE

Bonhoeffer, Dietrich. *Discipleship*. Minneapolis: Fortress Press, 2003 (1937).

Spy Wednesday

Unholy Alliances

As we prepare to commemorate the Lord's crucifixion on Good Friday, it is crucial first to revisit the specific circumstances leading up to his arrest, trial, and eventual execution:

> *Then the leading priests and Pharisees called the high council together. "What are we going to do?" they asked each other. "This man certainly performs many miraculous signs. If we allow him to go on like this, soon everyone will believe in him. Then the Roman army will come and destroy both our Temple and our nation."*
>
> *Caiaphas, who was high priest at that time, said, "You don't know what you're talking about! You don't realize that it's better for you that one man should die for the people than for the whole nation to be destroyed."*
>
> *He did not say this on his own; as high priest at that time he was led to prophesy that Jesus would die for the entire nation. And not only for that nation, but to bring together and unite all the children of God scattered around the world. So from that time on, the Jewish leaders began to plot Jesus's death.*
>
> —John 11:47–53 (NLT)

> *The Festival of Unleavened Bread, which is also called Passover, was approaching. The leading priests and teachers of religious law were plotting how to kill Jesus, but they were afraid of the people's reaction. Then Satan entered into Judas Iscariot, who was one of the twelve disciples, and he went to the leading priests and captains of the Temple guard to discuss the best way to betray Jesus to them. They were delighted, and they promised to give him money. So he*

> *agreed and began looking for an opportunity to betray Jesus so they could arrest him when the crowds weren't around.*
>
> —Luke 22:1–6 (NLT)

There exists a profound irony in the unlikely alliance formed between Judas Iscariot, for whom there are good reasons to believe held insurrectionist sympathies, and Caiaphas, a key collaborator (as high priest) within the Roman imperial matrix of control.[1] Each for their own reasons—be it disillusionment, survival, or greed—rejected Jesus and the cruciform way of life he modeled. Jesus lived his entire life in light of the cross. Yet, the cold utilitarian calculus leading to his execution nevertheless stands condemned. Ultimately, Jesus fell victim to an unholy marriage of religion, violent power, collective self-interest, and greed—a "Babylonian synthesis" condemned throughout the pages of Scripture. And, I can't help but draw contemporary parallels. Of the biblical challenge to this ungodly synthesis, comparative theologian Ida Glaser writes,

> [The New Testament] challenges all religions: it shatters ties between religion and territory, and between religion and power, even more strongly than did the exile. It also shatters the ties between religion and the Jewish people and their culture. These are the ties that support the dangerous triangle of people, power, and land that has always characterized so much religion. It is the cross that shatters them.[2]

To which she adds,

> "It shows weakness as true power, and it inaugurates a people whose identity does not depend on state or land. It points to a new creation, in which people will live in a new land, with God as their king."[3]

Jesus continuously disrupted and denounced this lethal alliance as it found expression within his first-century, ethno-religious community and, as a result, would incur the wrath of its leaders. Consistently rejecting, however, the dual temptations of both imperial compromise and armed rebellion, Jesus models for us the narrow path of self-sacrificial, non-violent, redemptive love. And, to reiterate, this love culminates in his unjust death on the

---

1. Horsely, "High Priests," 24; Hagner, *Matthew 14–28*, 754.
2. Glaser, The Bible and Other Faiths, Chap. 10.
3. Glaser, *The Bible and Other Faiths,* Chap. 10.

cross, where an instrument of imperial domination becomes the ultimate symbol of divine love and the power-reversing means by which God reigns.[4]

REFLECT

- What, in your own words, contributed to the arrest, trial, and execution of Jesus? What led Judas to betray Jesus? Why did the religious leaders seek his assassination?
- What is so deadly about "the dangerous triangle of people, power, and land that has always characterized so much religion?" Can you think of any modern-day examples of such unholy alliances?

PRAY

> We praise you, Almighty God, for your elect, the prophets and martyrs of humanity, who gave their thoughts and prayers and agonies for the truth of God and the freedom of the people. We praise you that amid loneliness and the contempt of men, in poverty and imprisonment, when they were condemned by the laws of the mighty and buffeted on the scaffold, you upheld them by your spirit in loyalty to your holy cause. Our hearts break within us as we follow the bleeding feet of Christ down through the centuries, and count the mounts of anguish on which he was crucified anew in his prophets and the true apostles of his spirit. Help us to forgive those who did it, for some truly thought they were serving you when they suppressed the light, but save us from the same mistake!
>
> Grant us an unerring instinct for what is right and true, and a swift sympathy to divine those who truly love and serve the people. Suffer us not by thoughtless condemnation or selfish opposition to weaken the arm and chill the spirit of those who strive for the redemption of humankind. May we never bring upon us the blood of all the righteous by renewing the spirit of those who persecuted them in the past. Grant us rather that we, too, may be counted in the chosen band of those who have given their life as a ransom for the many. Send us forth with the pathfinders of humanity to lead your people another day's march toward the land of promise. And if we, too, must suffer loss, and drink the bitter pool of misunderstanding and scorn, uphold us by your spirit in steadfastness and joy because we are found worthy to share in the work and the reward of Jesus and all the saints.

---

4. Ramachandra, *Gods that Fail*, 184–185.

> Serving a Crucified King
>
> —Walter Rauschenbusch (1910)

EXPLORE

DeSilva, David A. *Unholy Allegiances: Heeding Revelation's Warning.* Peabody: Hendrickson Publishing, 2013.

Glaser, Ida. *The Bible and Other Faiths: What Does the Lord Require of Us?* Carlisle: Langham Global Library, 2012.

Maundy Thursday

By the Sword

From Jesus's last supper with his disciples and the cleansing of their feet to the arrest and twin trials of Jesus, Maundy Thursday is a day of solemn remembrance. Today, we reflect upon the following incident from the Garden of Gethsemane:

> While he was still speaking, Judas, one of the Twelve, arrived. With him was a large crowd armed with swords and clubs, sent from the chief priests and the elders of the people. Now the betrayer had arranged a signal with them: "The one I kiss is the man; arrest him."
>
> Going at once to Jesus, Judas said, "Greetings, Rabbi!" and kissed him.
>
> Jesus replied, "Do what you came for, friend."
>
> Then the men stepped forward, seized Jesus and arrested him. With that, one of Jesus's companions reached for his sword, drew it out and struck the servant of the high priest, cutting off his ear. "Put your sword back in its place," Jesus said to him, "for all who draw the sword will die by the sword. Do you think I cannot call on my Father, and he will at once put at my disposal more than twelve legions of angels? But how then would the Scriptures be fulfilled that say it must happen in this way?"
>
> In that hour Jesus said to the crowd, "Am I leading a rebellion, that you have come out with swords and clubs to capture me? Every day I sat in the temple courts teaching, and you did not arrest me. But this has all taken place that the writings of the prophets might be fulfilled."
>
> Then all the disciples deserted him and fled.
>
> —Matthew 26:47–56 (NIV)

A few years ago, I was watching a Star Wars movie with my eldest son. Midway through the film he turned to me to express just how distressed he was by the high prevalence of storm trooper deaths. I couldn't help but smile and pray that he never outgrows such open-hearted empathy for all of God's children. As the footsoldiers of an evil empire (quite literally dehumanized, homogenized, and demonized behind a sterile white uniform), we generally think nothing of their deaths. Unfortunately, we too often divide the world in such a way between good guy and bad that it becomes the paradigm through which we interpret our interactions with others. We observe this time and again with regard to partisan polarization, sectarian tribalism, and nationalist chauvinism.

Our "good violence" is always justified, while the "bad guys" are forever deserving of their fate. Our dead, our "patriots and martyrs," are always reported upon and memorialized, whilst the victims of our aggression are conveniently undercounted or ignored. Meanwhile, it is forgotten that the ones with the guns are often just kids, victims themselves of the violent machinery and mythology of both empire and resistance alike. It's a tragic symptom of this sinful world that those who live by the sword die by it. Jesus's kingdom vision, however, is much greater. For "the line separating good from evil," Aleksandr Solzhenitsyn reminds us, "passes not through states, nor between classes, nor between political parties either—but right through every human heart."[1] Because, as the apostle writes, "our struggle is not against flesh and blood, but against the rulers, against the authorities, against the powers of this dark world and against the spiritual forces of evil in the heavenly realms."[2]

REFLECT

- Imagine yourself in the garden with Jesus and the disciples. How do you imagine you would have reacted to the arrest of Jesus? Why does Jesus allow himself to be arrested?

- Reflect on Jesus's declaration that "all who draw the sword will die by the sword?" What does he mean by such a statement? What are the implications for your context today?

---

1. Solzhenitsyn, *Gulag Archipelago*, Chap. 4.1.
2. Ephesians 6:12 (NIV)

PRAY

Our Father, we look back on the years that are gone and shame and sorrow come upon us, for the harm we have done to others rises up in our memory to accuse us. Some we have seared with the fire of our lust, and some we have scorched by the heart of our anger. In some we helped to quench the glow of young ideals by our selfish pride and craft, and in some we have nipped the opening bloom of faith by the frost of our unbelief. We might have followed your blessed footsteps, O Christ, binding up the bruised hearts of our brothers and sisters and guiding the wayward passions of the young to firmer adulthood. Instead, there are poor hearts now broken and darkened because they encountered us on the way, and some perhaps remember us only as the beginning of their misery or sin.

O God, we know that all our prayers can never bring back the past, and no tears can wash out the red marks with which we have scarred some life that stands before our memory with accusing eyes. Grant that at least a humble and pure life may grow out of our late contrition, that in the brief days still left to us we may comfort and heal where we have scorned and crushed. Change us by the power of your saving grace from sources of evil into forces for good, that with all our strength we may fight the wrongs we have aided, and aid the right we have clogged. Grant us this, for every soul that has stumbled or fallen through us, we may bring to you some other weak or despairing one, whose strength has been renewed by our love, that so the face of your Christ may smile upon us and the light within us may shine undimmed.

—Walter Rauschenbusch (1910)

EXPLORE

Sprinkle, Preston. *Nonviolence: The Revolutionary Way of Jesus.* Revised Edition. Colorado Springs: David C. Cook, 2021.

Good Friday

The Crucified King

AFTER A MOMENTARY SILENCE, MEDITATE upon the passion of our king and savior Jesus Christ:

> Some of the governor's soldiers took Jesus into their headquarters and called out the entire regiment. They stripped him and put a scarlet robe on him. They wove thorn branches into a crown and put it on his head, and they placed a reed stick in his right hand as a scepter. Then they knelt before him in mockery and taunted, "Hail! King of the Jews!" And they spit on him and grabbed the stick and struck him on the head with it. When they were finally tired of mocking him, they took off the robe and put his own clothes on him again. Then they led him away to be crucified.
>
> Along the way, they came across a man named Simon, who was from Cyrene, and the soldiers forced him to carry Jesus's cross. And they went out to a place called Golgotha (which means "Place of the Skull"). The soldiers gave Jesus wine mixed with bitter gall, but when he had tasted it, he refused to drink it.
>
> After they had nailed him to the cross, the soldiers gambled for his clothes by throwing dice. Then they sat around and kept guard as he hung there. A sign was fastened above Jesus's head, announcing the charge against him. It read: "This is Jesus, the King of the Jews." Two revolutionaries were crucified with him, one on his right and one on his left.
>
> The people passing by shouted abuse, shaking their heads in mockery. "Look at you now!" they yelled at him. "You said you were going to destroy the Temple and rebuild it in three days. Well then, if you are the Son of God, save yourself and come down from the cross!"

The Crucified King

The leading priests, the teachers of religious law, and the elders also mocked Jesus. "He saved others," they scoffed, "but he can't save himself! So he is the King of Israel, is he? Let him come down from the cross right now, and we will believe in him! He trusted God, so let God rescue him now if he wants him! For he said, 'I am the Son of God.'" Even the revolutionaries who were crucified with him ridiculed him in the same way.

At noon, darkness fell across the whole land until three o'clock. At about three o'clock, Jesus called out with a loud voice, "Eli, Eli, lema sabachthani?" which means "My God, my God, why have you abandoned me?"

Some of the bystanders misunderstood and thought he was calling for the prophet Elijah. One of them ran and filled a sponge with sour wine, holding it up to him on a reed stick so he could drink. But the rest said, "Wait! Let's see whether Elijah comes to save him."

Then Jesus shouted out again, and he released his spirit. At that moment the curtain in the sanctuary of the Temple was torn in two, from top to bottom. The earth shook, rocks split apart, and tombs opened. The bodies of many godly men and women who had died were raised from the dead. They left the cemetery after Jesus's resurrection, went into the holy city of Jerusalem, and appeared to many people.

The Roman officer and the other soldiers at the crucifixion were terrified by the earthquake and all that had happened. They said, "This man truly was the Son of God!"

And many women who had come from Galilee with Jesus to care for him were watching from a distance. Among them were Mary Magdalene, Mary (the mother of James and Joseph), and the mother of James and John, the sons of Zebedee.

—Matthew 27:27–56 (NLT)

REFLECT

Meditate on Christ's humiliation and execution for a few minutes in silence. Reflect upon true versus false notions of kingship, authority, power, faith, and what it means to reign by way of cross. Slowly read through the passage again, focusing on the section that convicts you the most or upon the concept you find most troubling. Pray over it. Ask the Lord to guide and direct you with regard to how he might be speaking through it to you in this moment. Ask for guidance and direction as to how you might not only believe but follow in the example of Jesus, to carry your own cross in a contemporary world awash with exploitation, violence, humiliation, and pain.

PRAY

God, the great Redeemer of humankind, our hearts are tender in the thought of you, for in all the affliction of our race you have been afflicted, and in the sufferings of your people it was your body that was crucified. You have been wounded by our transgressions and bruised by our iniquities, and all our sins are laid at last on you. Amid the groaning of creation we behold your spirit in travail until the children of God shall be born in freedom and holiness. We pray, O Lord, for the graces of a pure and holy life that we may no longer add to the dark weight of the world's sin that is laid upon you, but may share with you in your redemptive work.

As we have thirsted with evil passions to the destruction of women and men, do fill us now with hunger and thirst for justice that we may bear glad tidings to the poor and set at liberty all who are in the prison-house of want and sin. Lay your spirit upon us and inspire us with a passion of Christ-like love that we may join our lives to the weak and oppressed and may strengthen their cause by bearing their sorrows. And if the evil that is threatened turns to smite us and if we must learn the dark malignity of sinful power, comfort us by the thought that thus we are bearing in our body the marks of Jesus, and that only those who share in his free sacrifice shall feel the plenitude of your life. Help us in practice to carry forward the eternal cross of Christ, counting it joy if we, too, are sown as grains of wheat in the furrows of the world, for only by the agony of the righteous comes redemption.

—Walter Rauschenbusch (1910)

EXPLORE

Endo, Shusaku. *Silence: A Novel*. New York: Taplinger Publishing Company, 1969.

Green, Joel B., and Mark D. Baker. *Recovering the Scandal of the Cross: Atonement in New Testament and Contemporary Contexts*. Second Edition. Downers Grove: IVP Academic, 2011.

Great and Holy Saturday

I Saw a Lamb

APOCALYPSE—RATHER THAN DENOTING A CATACLYSMIC end-of-days confrontation between the forces of good and evil—refers to the revealing or unveiling of that which was heretofore hidden or unknown. As such, the great apocalyptic literature of Scripture works to draw back the curtain of heaven, allowing the prophet to understand and report upon the true nature of historical events as seen from above (rather than below). It shows us that God is sovereign and in control, even though everything around us may appear hopeless and lost. Here, John presents us with a vision of the throne room of heaven:

> Then I saw a scroll in the right hand of the one who was sitting on the throne. There was writing on the inside and the outside of the scroll, and it was sealed with seven seals. And I saw a strong angel, who shouted with a loud voice: "Who is worthy to break the seals on this scroll and open it?" But no one in heaven or on earth or under the earth was able to open the scroll and read it.
>
> Then I began to weep bitterly because no one was found worthy to open the scroll and read it. But one of the twenty-four elders said to me, "Stop weeping! Look, the Lion of the tribe of Judah, the Root of David, has won the victory. He is worthy to open the scroll and its seven seals."
>
> Then I saw a Lamb that looked as if it had been slaughtered, but it was now standing between the throne and the four living beings and among the twenty-four elders. He had seven horns and seven

> *eyes, which represent the sevenfold Spirit of God that is sent out into every part of the earth. He stepped forward and took the scroll from the right hand of the one sitting on the throne. And when he took the scroll, the four living beings and the twenty-four elders fell down before the Lamb. Each one had a harp, and they held gold bowls filled with incense, which are the prayers of God's people.*
>
> *And they sang a new song with these words: "You are worthy to take the scroll and break its seals and open it. For you were slaughtered, and your blood has ransomed people for God from every tribe and language and people and nation. And you have caused them to become a kingdom of priests for our God. And they will reign on the earth."*
>
> *Then I looked again, and I heard the voices of thousands and millions of angels around the throne and of the living beings and the elders. And they sang in a mighty chorus: "Worthy is the Lamb who was slaughtered—to receive power and riches and wisdom and strength and honor and glory and blessing."*
>
> *And then I heard every creature in heaven and on earth and under the earth and in the sea. They sang: "Blessing and honor and glory and power belong to the one sitting on the throne and to the Lamb forever and ever."*
>
> *And the four living beings said, "Amen!" And the twenty-four elders fell down and worshiped the Lamb.*
>
> —Revelation 5:1–14 (NLT)

Standing above and against all imperial pretenders ancient or modern is Jesus, not Caesar, who reigns as king. Yet the Lion of Judah reigns, not through the power of domination and might, but as the humiliated lamb who was slain and whose sacrificial blood would prove more powerful than mighty pharaoh in all of his destructive, imperial grandeur. The messiah reigns with bloody robes and a crown of thorns. Residing, therefore, at the very heart of the Christian story is the complete redefinition and total rejection of power as typically practiced. Instead, true power is found on the cross, in Christ's willingness and ability to take upon and absorb within himself all of the cruelty, humiliation, and death-dealing violence that empire has to offer. "All our collective human rebellion was poured out on him,"[1] Vinoth Ramachandra tells us.

> Indeed he allowed evil to do its worst to him. Paradoxically, the point of apparent defeat became the moment of greatest triumph. It was the victory of divine weakness over human strength, of the

---

1. Ramachandra, *Gods that Fail*, 184.

word of truth over the machinations of power, of self-surrendering love over self-grasping hate.[2]

Authentic kingship consists in self-sacrificial love. To reign with Christ is to follow his lead and carry our own cross in loving, sacrificial service to a world crying out for redemption and deliverance. Even as things look bleak, we act in hopeful anticipation of the coming resurrection.

REFLECT

- What is the relationship between Christ's "worthiness" and his death on the cross? What does it mean for Jesus to "to reign with bloody robes"?
- What does it mean for you and your faith community to serve Jesus as the crucified king, the lamb who was slain?

PRAY

Let us proclaim, together with the multitudes of heaven, our praises to the crucified king.

> *And they sang a new song with these words: "You are worthy to take the scroll and break its seals and open it. For you were slaughtered, and your blood has ransomed people for God from every tribe and language and people and nation. And you have caused them to become a kingdom of priests for our God. And they will reign on the earth."*
>
> *Then I looked again, and I heard the voices of thousands and millions of angels around the throne and of the living beings and the elders. And they sang in a mighty chorus: "Worthy is the Lamb who was slaughtered—to receive power and riches and wisdom and strength and honor and glory and blessing."*
>
> *And then I heard every creature in heaven and on earth and under the earth and in the sea. They sang: "Blessing and honor and glory and power belong to the one sitting on the throne and to the Lamb forever and ever."*
>
> *And the four living beings said: "Amen!"*
>
> *And the twenty-four elders fell down and worshiped the Lamb.*
>
> —REVELATION 5:9–14 (NLT)

---

2. Ramachandra, *Gods that Fail*, 185.

EXPLORE

Collins, John J. *The Apocalyptic Imagination: An Introduction to Jewish Apocalyptic Literature* Third Edition. Grand Rapids: Eerdmans, 2016.

DeSilva, David A. *Discovering Revelation: Content, Interpretation, Reception.* Grand Rapids: Eerdmans, 2021.

Easter Sunday

New Creation

THIS IS THE STORY OF new creation's birth, of the resurrection of Jesus Christ:

> On the first day of the week, very early in the morning, the women took the spices they had prepared and went to the tomb. They found the stone rolled away from the tomb, but when they entered, they did not find the body of the Lord Jesus. While they were wondering about this, suddenly two men in clothes that gleamed like lightning stood beside them. In their fright the women bowed down with their faces to the ground, but the men said to them, "Why do you look for the living among the dead? He is not here; he has risen! Remember how he told you, while he was still with you in Galilee: 'The Son of Man must be delivered over to the hands of sinners, be crucified and on the third day be raised again.'"
>
> Then they remembered his words. When they came back from the tomb, they told all these things to the Eleven and to all the others. It was Mary Magdalene, Joanna, Mary the mother of James, and the others with them who told this to the apostles. But they did not believe the women, because their words seemed to them like nonsense. Peter, however, got up and ran to the tomb.
>
> —LUKE 24:1–12 (NIV)

It must be emphasized that the first witnesses to and proclaimers of the good news of the resurrection were the women. This is no accident. Luke even makes a point of highlighting the fact that the very first gospel presentation was dismissed by the men, an unfortunately all too common occurrence in this day and age as well. Jesus, however, centers and amplifies the stories of women at critical moments throughout his story, beginning to end, and entrusts them with the preaching of the great news to the other disciples.

Ultimately, what the resurrection represents is the vindication of Christ before those earthen embodiments of the beast, those brokers of wealth, power, and violence at whose hands he was crucified. For in the resurrection, death has lost its sting. The authorities, having played their hand, exhausted the only true power they had and lost the war. As a result, our own hope for resurrection frees us to give generously rather than hoard, lay down our arms in the pursuit of peace, and speak truth to the lies of power. In the words of N. T. Wright,

> What we are witnessing in the resurrection stories . . . is *the birth of new creation*. The power that has tyrannized the old creation has been broken, defeated, overthrown. *God's kingdom is now launched, and launched in power and glory, on earth as in heaven.* This is what Jesus said would happen within the lifetime of his hearers. A new power is let loose in the world, the power to remake what was broken, to heal what was diseased, to restore what was lost.[1]

To which he adds, "New creation has begun; and its motivating power is love."[2]

REFLECT

- How and in what ways does the resurrection represent Christ's vindication before and ultimate victory over the power of evil?
- What does it look like to live as people of the new creation, in the midst of the old creation?

PRAY

> *Christ, you have bidden us pray for the coming of your Father's kingdom, in which his righteous will shall be done on earth. We have treasured your words, but we have forgotten their meaning, and your great hope has grown dim in your church. We bless you for the inspired souls of all ages who saw afar the shining city of God, and by faith left the profit of the present to follow their vision. We rejoice that today the hope of these lonely hearts is becoming the clear faith*

---

1. Wright, *Simply Jesus*, 193.
2. Wright, *Simply Jesus*, 194.

of millions. Help us, O Lord, in the courage of faith to seize what has now come so near, that the glad day of God may dawn at last. As we have mastered nature that we might gain wealth, help us now to master the social relations of humankind that we may gain justice and a world of brothers and sisters.

For what shall it profit our nation if it gain numbers and riches, and lose the sense of the living God and the joy of human siblinghood? Make us determined to live by truth and not by lies, to found our common life on the eternal foundations of righteousness and love, and no longer to prop up the tottering house of wrong by legalized cruelty and force. Help us to make the welfare of all the supreme law of our land, that so our commonwealth may be built strong and secure on the love of all its citizens. Cast down the throne of Mammon who ever grinds the life of women and men, and set up your throne, O Christ, for you died that people might live. Show your erring children at last the way from the City of Destruction to the City of Love, and fulfil the longings of the prophets of humanity. Our master, once more we make your faith our prayer: "Thy kingdom Come! They will on earth be done!"

—Walter Rauschenbusch (1910)

EXPLORE

Wright, N. T. *Simply Jesus: A New Vision of Who He Was, What He Did, and Why It Matters.* New York: HarperCollins, 2011.

Appendix

ADAPTING TO A LONGER WEEKLY FORMAT

I HAVE INCLUDED WITHIN this appendix a very brief introduction to four great methodologies for adapting these lessons to a longer weekly format. They are

- Inductive Bible Study
- Discovery Bible Study
- HBLT ("Hook, Book, Look, Took")
- *Lectio Divina*

INDUCTIVE BIBLE STUDY

At its most basic, Inductive Bible Study consists of three sequential yet interrelated movements, each centered upon a specific question brought to a particular text of Scripture. These include

- *Observation*: "What does a text say?"
- *Interpretation*: "What does the text mean?"
- *Application*: "How is God inviting us to respond?"

It is quite amazing to see just how much substantive discussion can result from these three questions alone, though additional follow-up questions can be added as they relate to each of the three movements. This specific collection of meditations is curated, and therefore not technically inductive; however, each lesson can be easily adapted for group use by incorporating inductive questions focused on observation, interpretation, and application.

Appendix

For additional information:

- Olesberg, Lindsay. *The Bible Study Handbook: A Comprehensive Guide to an Essential Practice.* Downers Grove: Intervarsity, 2012.
- Wilhoit, James C., and Leland Ryken. *Effective Bible Teaching.* Second Edition. Grand Rapids: Baker Academic, 2012.
- Intervarsity Christian Fellowship: howto.bible

DISCOVERY BIBLE STUDY

The genius behind the Discovery Bible Study method is its simplicity and missional reproducibility. Designed to facilitate the organic growth of discipleship movements, most especially among new or non-believers, and to get people as quickly as possible into Scripture, all one needs is a copy of the Bible, a group facilitator, and the following template (as adapted from: www.dbsguide.org). Each participant answers the following questions as time permits:

- *Talk*: What are you thankful for? What is causing you stress? Who needs our help? How can this group help them?
- *Look Back*: Retell story from the previous meeting. What did you do differently because of this story? Who did you tell and what was the reaction?
- *Read & Re-Tell*: One person reads the Bible passage out loud, and the rest follow along. Someone else retells the passage by memory, if possible. Others can fill in what is missing.
- *Look*: Read the passage again. Discuss what this passage says about God, Jesus, or God's plan.
- *Look Again*: Read the passage once more. Discuss what this passage says about humans.
- *Inside Me*: According to this study, what am I doing well? What do I need to change?
- *Who Else?* Who needs to hear this story? How can I tell them? Who can I invite to study the Bible?

Appendix

The passages and pre-written questions in this collection can be easily adapted to the above template.

For additional information:

- Watson, David, and Paul Watson. *Contagious Disciple Making: Leading Others on a Journey of Discovery.* Nashville: Thomas Nelson, 2014.
- Discovery Bible Study: www.dbsguide.org.

HBLT ("HOOK, BOOK, LOOK, TOOK")

For the purposes of constructing a lesson within a more didactic context like adult Sunday school, it is hard to go wrong with the "Hook, Book, Look, Took" method. First set forth by Lawrence O. Richards in his book, *Creative Bible Teaching*, I have found this method to be incredibly helpful (after learning about it myself from theological education specialist Perry Shaw).

- *Hook* contains a short introduction meant to capture the attention of your listeners, engaging their natural curiosity to "hook" them into your lesson.
- *Book* is a time for looking together at a text of Scripture (or your primary subject matter if you are teaching in a different context) to understand its meaning and message, as situated within its own literary and historical context.
- *Look* consists of an exploration as to how the passage applies to our present context and daily lives.
- *Took* gives to participants a tangible lesson or action to take with them for the coming week as they leave the gathering.

"Hook, Book, Look, Took" is a simple yet remarkably successful method for crafting individual lessons for engaging the listener's "head, hands, and heart." This may take a bit of creativity on the part of the instructor, but the meditations contained in this collection can serve as a solid basis for constructing such lessons.

Appendix

For additional information:

- Richards, Lawrence O., and Gary J. Bredfeldt. *Creative Bible Teaching*. Revised and Updated. Chicago: Moody Publishers, 2020.
- Shaw, Perry. *Transforming Theological Education: A Practical Handbook for Integrative Learning*. ICETE Series. Carlisle: Langham Global Library, 2014.

LECTIO DIVINA

A contemplative monastic practice established by Benedict of Nursia in the sixth century and performed to this day by Protestant and Catholic alike, *lectio divina* ("divine reading") combines Scripture reading, mediation, and prayer as a means of hearing God speak to us through his holy word in the moment. Unapologetically subjective, *lectio divina* traditionally consists of a series of sequential movements, and while there are a number of different models, the following is adapted from the version I first learned from Richard Peace as a student at Fuller Theological Seminary:

- *Prepare*: Everyone should sit comfortably, regulate their breathing, and ask God to speak to them through the reading. Everyone but the reader should close their eyes.
- *Listen*: Read the passage twice. After a brief silence, the facilitator asks each person to share the word or phrase that most struck them during the reading. No explanation should be offered at this point.
- *Meditate*: A different person will read the passage for a third time. Then, everyone should silently reflect for a couple minutes and consider how that word or phrase intersects with their lives. Afterwards, each person should explain—in one to two sentences max—the connection they see.
- *Invite*: The text is read for a fourth time by a different person, followed by an additional period of silent reflection wherein each person is invited to ask themselves whether they are being invited to do something. Afterwards, each person shares what they think that invitation might be.

Appendix

Then, the session concludes with a time of prayer, followed by an optional time for open discussion.

For additional information:

- Peace, Richard. *Contemplative Bible Reading: Experiencing God through Scripture.* Colorado Springs: Navpress, 1998.
- Vest, Norvene. *Gathered in the Word: Praying the Scripture in Small Groups.* Nashville: Upper Room, 2019.

Bibliography

TO EXPLORE FURTHER

Accad, Martin. "Christian Attitudes toward Islam and Muslims: A Kerygmatic Approach." In *Toward Respectful Understanding and Witness among Muslims: Essays in Honor of J. Dudley Woodberry*, edited by Evelyne Reisacher et al., Chapter 1. Pasadena: William Carey, 2012. Kindle.

Accad, Martin, and Jonathan Andrews, eds. *The Religious Other: A Biblical Understanding of Islam, the Qur'an, and Muhammad*. Institute of Middle East Studies Series. Carlisle: Langham Global Library, 2020.

Ambrose of Milan. "On Naboth." *Divine Will*. Accessed July 29, 2021. https://hymnsandchants.com/Texts/Sermons/Ambrose/OnNaboth.htm.

Andrews, Jonathan, ed. *The Church in Disorienting Times: Leading Prophetically through Adversity*. Institute of Middle East Studies Series. Carlisle: Langham Global Library, 2018.

———, ed. Andrews. *The Missiology behind the Story: Voices from the Arab World*. The Institute of Middle East Studies Series. Carlisle: Langham Global Library, 2019.

Arrupe, Pedro. "On Poverty, Work, and Common Life." In *Challenge to Religious Life Today: Selected Letters and Addresses—I*, edited by Jerome Aixala, 11–34. St. Louis: The Institute of Jesuit Sources, 1979.

Bailey, Kenneth E. *Jesus through Middle Eastern Eyes: Cultural Studies in the Gospels*. Downers Grove: IVP Academic, 2009.

Bible Project. "Heaven & Earth." Accessed July 15, 2021. https://bibleproject.com/explore/heaven-earth/.

Bonhoeffer, Dietrich. *Discipleship*. Minneapolis: Fortress, 2003 (1937).

Boyle, Gregory. *Tattoos on the Heart: The Power of Boundless Compassion*. New York: Free, 2011.

Bruce, F. F. *New Testament Development of Old Testament Themes*. Milton Keynes: Paternoster, 1968.

Brueggemann, Walter. *From Judgment to Hope: A Study on the Prophets*. Louisville: Westminster John Knox, 2019.

———. *Interrupting Silence: God's Command to Speak Out*. Louisville: Westminster John Knox, 2018.

———. *Materiality as Resistance: Five Elements for Moral Action in the Real World*. Louisville: Westminster John Knox, 2020.

Bunge, Marcia J., ed. *The Child in the Bible*. Grand Rapids: Eerdmans, 2008.

Bibliography

———, ed. *The Child in Christian Thought*. Grand Rapids: Eerdmans, 2001.
Buttry, Daniel L. *Peace Warrior: A Memoir from the Front*. Macon: Mercer University Press, 2013.
Buttry, Sharon A., and Dan L. Buttry. *Daughters of Rizpah: Nonviolence and the Transformation of Trauma*. Eugene: Cascade, 2020.
Câmara, Hélder. *Dom Hélder Câmara: Essential Writings*. Edited by Francis McDonagh. Maryknoll: Orbis, 2009.
Chapman, Colin. *Whose Holy City? Jerusalem and the Future of Peace in the Middle East*. Grand Rapids: Baker, 2004.
Collins, John J. *The Apocalyptic Imagination: An Introduction to Jewish Apocalyptic Literature*. Third Edition. Grand Rapids: Eerdmans, 2016.
Daniels, T. Scott. *Embracing Exile: Living Faithfully as God's Unique People in the World*. Kansas City: Nazarene, 2017.
Das, Rupen. *Compassion and the Mission of God: Revealing the Invisible Kingdom*. Carlisle: Langham Global Library, 2016.
Das, Rupen, and Brent Hamoud. *Strangers in the Kingdom: Ministering to Refugees, Migrants and the Stateless*. Carlisle: Langham Global Library, 2017.
DeSilva, David A. *Discovering Revelation: Content, Interpretation, Reception*. Grand Rapids: Eerdmans, 2021.
———. *Honor, Patronage, Kinship & Purity: Unlocking New Testament Culture*. Downers Grove: IVP Academic, 2012.
———. *Unholy Allegiances: Heeding Revelation's Warning*. Peabody: Hendrickson, 2013.
Discovery Bible Study. "Discovery Bible Study." Accessed July 15, 2021. www.dbsguide.org.
Endo, Shusaku. *Silence: A Novel*. New York: Taplinger, 1969.
Fiske, Alan Page, and Tage Shakti Rai. *Virtuous Violence: Hurting and Killing to Create, Sustain, End, and Honor Social Relationships*. Cambridge: Cambridge University Press, 2014.
Glaser, Ida. *The Bible and Other Faiths: What Does the Lord Require of Us?* Carlisle: Langham Global Library, 2012. Kindle.
Goldingay, John. *The Theology of the Book of Isaiah*. Downers Grove: IVP Academic, 2014.
Gorman, Michael J. *Reading Revelation Responsibly: Uncivil Worship and Witness: Following the Lamb into the New Creation*. Eugene: Cascade, 2011. Kindle.
Gowan, Donald E. *The Theology of the Prophetic Books: The Death & Resurrection of Israel*. Louisville: Westminster John Knox, 1998.
Green, Joel B., and Mark D. Baker. *Recovering the Scandal of the Cross: Atonement in New Testament and Contemporary Contexts*. Second Edition. Downers Grove: IVP Academic, 2011.
Groody, Daniel G. *Globalization, Spirituality, and Justice: Navigating a Path to Peace*. Revised Edition. Maryknoll: Orbis, 2015. Kindle.
Gushee, David P., and Reggie L. Williams, eds. *Justice and the Way of Jesus: Christian Ethics and the Incarnational Discipleship of Glen Stassen*. Maryknoll: Orbis, 2020.
Gushee, David P., and Glen H. Stassen. *Kingdom Ethics: Following Jesus in Contemporary Context*. Second Edition. Grand Rapids: Eerdmans, 2016.
Haddad, Elie, and Jesse Steven Wheeler. "Jesus Christ, King and Caliph: The Writings of Glen Stassen and Our Middle Eastern Communities." *Christian Ethics Today* 22:4 (2014) 16–20.

Bibliography

Hagner, Donald A. *Matthew 1–13, Volume 33a*. Word Biblical Commentary. Nashville: Thomas Nelson, 1993.

———. *Matthew 14–28, Volume 33b*. Word Biblical Commentary. Grand Rapids: Zondervan, 1995.

Hauerwas, Stanley, and William H. Willimon. *Resident Aliens: Life in the Christian Colony*. Expanded Twenty-Fifth Anniversary Edition. Nashville: Abingdon, 2014.

Himes, Brant, M. *For a Better Worldliness: Abraham Kuyper, Dietrich Bonhoeffer, and Discipleship for the Common Good*. Eugene: Pickwick, 2019.

Horsely, Richard A. "High Priests and the Politics of Roman Palestine: A Contextual Analysis of the Evidence in Joseph." *Journal for the Study of Judaism* 17 (1986) 23–55.

Hudson, Michael. *. . . and forgive them their debts: Lending, Foreclosure and Redemption from Bronze Age Finance to the Jubilee Year*. Dresden: ISLET-Verlag, 2018.

Intervarsity Christian Fellowship. "Leading a Group." Accessed July 15, 2021. http://howto.bible/content/leading-group.

Jones, Tony. *The Teaching of the Twelve: Believing & Practicing the Primitive Christianity of the Ancient Didache Community*. Brewster: Paraclete, 2009.

Kaemingk, Matthew, and Cory B. Willson. *Work and Worship: Reconnecting Our Labor and Liturgy*. Grand Rapids: Baker Academic, 2020.

Kärkkäinen, Veli-Matti. *Christ and Reconciliation: A Constructive Christian Theology for the Pluralistic World, vol. 1*. Grand Rapids: Eerdmans, 2013.

Kashouh, Hikmat. *Following Jesus in Turbulent Times: Disciple-Making in the Arab World*. Carlisle: Langham Global Library, 2018.

Kuhn, Michael F. *God Is One: A Christian Defence of Divine Unity in the Muslim Golden Age*. Carlisle: Langham Global Library, 2019.

Labberton, Mark. *The Dangerous Act of Loving Your Neighbor: Seeing Others through the Eyes of Jesus*. Downers Grove: Intervarsity, 2010.

———. *The Dangerous Act of Worship: Living God's Call to Justice*. Downers Grove: Intervarsity, 2007.

Ladd, George Eldon, and Donald A. Hagner. *A Theology of the New Testament*. Revised Edition. Grand Rapids: Eerdmans, 2010.

Lederach, John Paul. *Reconcile: Conflict Transformation for Ordinary Christians*. Harrisonburg: Herald, 2014.

Matthews McGinnis, Claire R. "Exodus as a 'Text of Terror' for Children." In *The Child in the Bible*, edited by Marcia J. Bunge, et al., 24–44. Grand Rapids: Eerdmans, 2008.

McConnell, Douglas, Jennifer Orona, and Paul Stockley, eds. *Understanding God's Heart for Children: Toward a Biblical Framework*. Milton Keynes: Authentic, 2007.

McCullough, Andy. *The Bethlehem Story: Mission and Justice in the Margins of the World*. Eugene: Resource, 2021.

McGuire, M. R. P. "De Nabuthae," *Patristic Studies*, vol. 15 (1927): 46–103. Quoted in Robert McAnally Adams, "Feast of Ambrose, Bishop of Milan, Teacher, 397," *CQOD* (December 7, 2018). http://www.cqod.com/index-12-07-18.html.

McKnight, Scot. *Sermon on the Mount*. The Story of God Bible Commentary 21. Grand Rapids: Zondervan Academic, 2013.

Migration Data Portal. Accessed July 13, 2021. https://migrationdataportal.org/.

Miller, Brandi. *Advent*. Seattle: Reclaiming My Theology, 2020.

Mouw, Richard J. *Abraham Kuyper: A Short and Personal Introduction*. Grand Rapids: Eerdmans, 2011. Kindle.

Bibliography

Munayer, Salim J., and Lisa Loden. *Through My Enemy's Eyes: Envisioning Reconciliation in Israel-Palestine*. Milton Keynes: Paternoster, 2014.

Myers, Bryant L. *Engaging Globalization: The Poor, Christian Mission, and Our Hyperconnected World*. Grand Rapids: Baker Academic, 2017.

———. *Walking with the Poor: Principles and Practices of Transformational Development*. Revised and Expanded Edition. Maryknoll: Orbis, 2011.

Nouwen, Henri J. M. *The Wounded Healer: Ministry in Contemporary Society*. New York: Doubleday, 1979.

Olesberg, Lindsay. *The Bible Study Handbook: A Comprehensive Guide to an Essential Practice*. Downers Grove: Intervarsity, 2012.

Paul VI. *Octogesima Adveniens: Apostolic Letter of Pope Paul VI*. Vatican City: Libreria Editrice Vaticana, 1971.

———. *Populorum Progressio: An Encyclical of Pope Paul VI on the Development of Peoples*. Vatican City: Libreria Editrice Vaticana, 1967.

Potts, J. Manning. *Prayers of the Early Church*. Nashville: The Upper Room, 1953.

Ramachandra, Vinoth. *Gods that Fail: Modern Idolatry and Christian Mission*. Revised Edition. Eugene: Wipf & Stock, 2016.

Ramachandra, Vinoth. *Subverting Global Myths: Theology and the Public Issues Shaping Our World*. Downers Grove: IVP Academic, 2008.

Rauschenbusch, Walter. *Christianity and the Social Crisis in the 21st Century: The Classic that Woke Up the Church*. San Francisco: HarperOne, 2009.

———. *For God and the People: Prayers of the Social Awakening*. Cleveland: Pilgrim, 1910.

Peace, Richard. *Contemplative Bible Reading: Experiencing God through Scripture*. Colorado Springs: Navpress, 1998.

Reimer, Johannes. *Missio Politica: The Mission of Church and Politics*. Carlisle: Langham Global Library, 2017.

Richards, Lawrence O., and Gary J. Bredfeldt. *Creative Bible Teaching*. Revised and Updated. Chicago: Moody, 2020.

Riddle, M. B., trans. "The Didache." In *Ante-Nicene Fathers, Volume 7*, edited by Alexander Roberts, James Donaldson, and A. Cleveland Coxe. Buffalo: Christian Literature, 1886.

Sarna, Nahum. *Understanding Genesis*. New York: Jewish Theological Seminary, 1966.

Sennott, Charles M. *The Body and the Blood: The Middle East's Vanishing Christians and the Possibility for Peace*. New York: Public Affairs, 2002.

Shaw, Karen L. H. *Wealth and Piety: Middle Eastern Perspectives for Expat Workers*. Pasadena: William Carey, 2018.

Shaw, Perry. *Transforming Theological Education: A Practical Handbook for Integrative Learning*. ICETE Series. Carlisle: Langham Global Library, 2014.

Smith, Kay Higuera, Jayachitra Lalitha, and L. Daniel Hawk, eds. *Evangelical Postcolonial Conversations: Global Awakenings in Theology and Praxis*. Downers Grove: IVP Academic, 2014.

Solzhenitsyn, Aleksandr. *The Gulag Archipelago: An Experiment in Literary Investigation*. Volume Two. New York: Harper Perennial, 2020. Kindle.

Sprinkle, Preston. *Nonviolence: The Revolutionary Way of Jesus*. Revised Edition. Colorado Springs: David C. Cook, 2021.

Stassen, Glen H. *A Thicker Jesus: Incarnational Discipleship in a Secular Age*. Louisville: Westminster John Knox, 2012.

Bibliography

———. *Living the Sermon on the Mount: A Practical Hope for Grace and Deliverance*. San Francisco: Jossey-Bass, 2006. Kindle.

Stassen, Glen H., Rodney L. Peterson, and Timothy A. Norton, eds. *Formation for Life: Just Peacemaking and Twenty-First-Century Discipleship*. Eugene: Pickwick, 2013.

Stearns, Richard. *The Hole in Our Gospel: What Does God Expect of Us? The Answer that Changed My Life and Might Just Change the World*. Tenth Anniversary Edition. Nashville: Thomas Nelson, 2019.

Strohl, Jane E. "The Child in Luther's Theology: 'For What Purpose Do We Older Folks, Exist, Other Than to Care for . . . the Young?'" In *The Child in Christian Thought*, edited by Marcia J. Bunge, 134–159. Grand Rapids: Eerdmans, 2001.

Tucker, Ruth A., and Walter Liefeld. *Daughters of the Church: Women and Ministry from New Testament Times to the Present*. Grand Rapids: Zondervan, 1987.

United Nations, Department of Economic and Social Affairs, Population Division (2019). *International Migration 2019: Report*. New York: United Nations, 2019.

Vest, Norvene. *Gathered in the Word: Praying the Scripture in Small Groups*. Nashville: Upper Room, 2019.

Volf, Miroslav. *Exclusion and Embrace: A Theological Exploration of Identity, Otherness, and Reconciliation*. Revised and Updated. Nashville: Abingdon, 2019.

———. *Free of Charge: Giving and Forgiving in a Culture Stripped of Grace*. Grand Rapids: Zondervan, 2006.

Walton, John H. *The Lost World of Genesis One: Ancient Cosmology and the Origins Debate*. Downers Grove: IVP Academic, 2010.

Walton, Jonathan P., Suzie Lahoud, and Sy Hoekstra, eds. *Keeping the Faith: Reflections on Politics & Christianity in the Era of Trump & Beyond*. Middletown: KTF, 2020.

Walton, Jonathan P. *Twelve Lies that Hold America Captive: And the Truth that Sets Us Free*. Downers Grove: Intervarsity, 2019.

Weaver, Dorothy Jean. *The Irony of Power: The Politics of God within Matthew's Narrative*. Eugene: Pickwick, 2017.

Watson, David, and Paul Watson. *Contagious Disciple Making: Leading Others on a Journey of Discovery*. Nashville: Thomas Nelson, 2014.

Wheeler, Jesse Steven. "Alternate Light: Christian Witness in Imitation of Christ." *The IMES Blog*. Arab Baptist Theological Seminary (2014). IMES.blog.

———. "Bad Theology Kills: How We Justify Killing Arabs." *The IMES Blog*. Arab Baptist Theological Seminary (2014). IMES.blog.

———. "Christ-Centered Witness and the Proper Use of Power." *The IMES Blog*. Arab Baptist Theological Seminary (2013). IMES.blog.

———. "Defacing the Image of God: The Children of War and Our Collective Human Failure." *The IMES Blog*. Arab Baptist Theological Seminary (2017). IMES.blog.

———. "Kerygmatic Peacebuilding (Part 2): What Does Peace Have to Do with the Gospel?" *The IMES Blog*. Arab Baptist Theological Seminary (2016). IMES.blog.

Wilhoit, James C., and Leland Ryken. *Effective Bible Teaching*. Second Edition. Grand Rapids: Baker Academic, 2012.

Wilson-Hartgrove, Johnathan. *Reconstructing the Gospel: Finding Freedom from Slaveholder Religion*. Downers Grove: Intervarsity, 2018.

Wright, Christopher J. H. *The Mission of God: Unlocking the Bible's Grand Narrative*. Downers Grove: IVP Academic, 2013.

Wright, N. T. *How God Became King: The Forgotten Story of the Gospels*. New York: HarperCollins, 2012.

Bibliography

———. *Simply Jesus: A New Vision of Who He Was, What He Did, and Why It Matters.* New York: Harper Collins, 2011.

———. *Surprised by Hope: Rethinking Heaven, the Resurrection, and the Mission of the Church.* New York: HarperCollins, 2009.

———. *The Lord and His Prayer.* Grand Rapids: Eerdmans, 2014.

www.ingramcontent.com/pod-product-compliance
Lightning Source LLC
Chambersburg PA
CBHW051057160426
43193CB00010B/1222